The Guru Method

WorkBook - Section III

For information contact:

GSMS Education Pty Ltd
P.O Box 3848
Marsfield NSW
2122
Australia

GAMSAT Practice Questions —Section III

Welcome to Workbook #2 – GAMSAT Practice Questions Section III. It will give you the opportunity to practice on "realistic" GAMSAT style questions. It consists of GAMSAT "Units" that are similar in style to GAMSAT questions.

The solutions are fully worked. There are FOUR sections; Biology, Physics, Organic Chemistry and General Chemistry.

Table of Contents

BIOLOGY: Unit 1

Questions 1–3

An electrocardiogram is a non-invasive test that records the electrical activity of the heart. The electrical activity is related to the impulses that travel through the heart that determine the heart's rate and rhythm. A diagram of a typical ECG is below. Each large square represents 200ms of time horizontally and 10 mV vertically. For each set of waves, the first wave (P) represents atrial contraction, the second wave (QRS) represents ventricular contraction, and the third wave (T) marks the return of the ventricles to their normal state.

ECG Trace

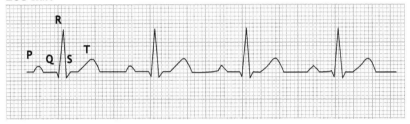

1. From this diagram, what is the heart rate?
   A   50 beats/min
   B   60 beats/min
   C   70 beats/min
   D   80 beats/min

2. How long is the systolic beat?
   A   0.35s
   B   0.15s
   C   3.5s
   D   1.5s

An ECG is a record of voltage and time. Metal silver/silver chloride electrodes are placed on the skin's surface in order to record the variations in the hearts voltage. Since voltage is just a separation of charge, at least two electrodes are needed to measure this separation as one lead will record the positive charge and the other the negative. In most:

3 What is the peak voltage at the skin's surface?

   A 0.20V

   B 0.26V

   C 0.026V

   D 0.022V

UNIT 2

Questions 4-7

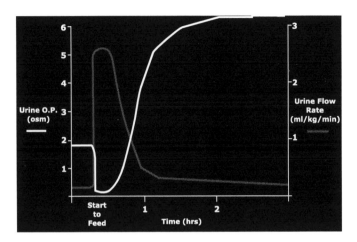

Vampire Bat Osmo-regulation

Adaptive modification of urinary output is easily illustrated with reference to Desmodus, the vampire bat. Prior to feeding, the bat renal system is in a "drought" condition, producing a low quantity of concentrated urine. When the bat consumes a blood meal, the system adapts to a "flood" condition, producing a large volume of dilute urine. Over the next hour or so, urine volume decreases while concentration increases up to 20 times that of plasma. This concentration increase is due to the high protein nature of the food; as it is processed, deamination results in the need to remove considerable quantities of urea, which causes the increase in urine osmo-concentration.

4. At what time point on the graph does the bat consume a blood meal?
   A ~1 hr
   B ~20 min
   C ~50 min
   D ~2 hr

5 When a vampire bat consumes a blood meal, the rapid ingestion of blood can result in a 30-40% increase in body weight which can hinder the bat's ability to fly. How does the bat counter this problem?

A The bat's urine flow reaches a maximum flow rate approximately 20 minutes after feeding

B The bat's urine flow reaches a maximum flow rate approximately 1 hr and 20 minutes after feeding

C The bat's urine osmo-concentration reaches a maximum approximately 20 minutes after feeding

D The bat's urine osmo-concentration reaches a maximum approximately 20 minutes after feeding

6 Flying increases evaporative water loss. How does the vampire bat offset this evaporative loss?

    A By eating only liquid meals

    B By ingesting mainly protein

    C By increasing urine output following feeding

    D By increasing urine concentration to a maximum within several hours following a feeding

7 Deamination of amino acids results in the conversion of the amino acid to waste products such as ammonia, urea, and uric acid. Why is it necessary for the bat to convert its waste products to urea instead of ammonia?

    A Urea is more soluble than ammonia and therefore easier to excrete

    B Ammonia is toxic and cannot be stored in high concentrations

    C Urea excretion assists with removing the large volumes of urine that are produced after feeding

    D Excreting ammonia requires a considerable amount of energy

UNIT 3

Questions 8–10

The most common forms of radiation include gamma rays, alpha rays, beta rays, x rays, and positrons. Radioactive elements are highly unstable and will undergo radioactive decay, emitting some forms of radiation and resulting in a change in energy state of the unstable nucleus. Nuclear medicine uses this principle because it is known that radiation can kill living cells, a fact which medicine uses to its advantage, using radiation to kill cancerous cells. In addition, radioactive atoms and pharmaceuticals are used in nuclear imaging procedures because they are attracted to specific tissue, organs, and bones and will emit certain forms of radiation that can be detected by a special camera.

<u>Alpha rays</u>-made of alpha particles (α), these are high speed helium nuclei produced in the nucleus during radioactive decay.

<u>Beta rays</u>-consist of beta particles (β), these are high speed electrons produced in the nucleus during radioactive decay. During basic beta decay, a neutron is turned into a proton and an electron (beta particle) is released.

<u>Gamma rays</u>(g)-does not consist of particles, it is similar to X-rays but of higher energy. During gamma decay, the nucleus falls down to a lower energy state and a photon (sometimes called a gamma particle) is released.

<u>X-rays</u>-energetic radiation emitted from atoms when an electron changes from a very high orbit to a very low orbit.

<u>Positrons</u>-like an electron, but with a positive charge. During positron emission, a proton is turned into a positron and a neutron and the positron is emitted.

8 Why are gamma rays used in nuclear imaging?
    A They do not carry a charge
    B They have higher energy than X-rays
    C They have the greatest penetrating ability of all the forms of radiation
    D They are the most stable form of radiation

9 What type of radioactive decay is occurring in the following reaction?

$H^3 \rightarrow He^3$ + radioactive particle

A Gamma decay

B Alpha decay

C Positron emission

D Beta decay

10 What would be the resulting molecule from an alpha decay of Plutonium-239?

$Pu^{239} \rightarrow U^x$ + alpha particle

A Uranium-235

B Uranium-236

C Uranium-237

D Uranium-238

UNIT 4

Questions 11–14

The radioactive half-life for a given radioisotope is physically determined and unaffected by the physical or chemical conditions around it. The half-life is the time it takes for a given radioactive isotope to lose half of its radioactivity. However, if that radioisotope is in a living organism it may be excreted so that it no longer is a source of radiation exposure to the organism. For a number of radioisotopes of particular medical interest, the rate of excretion has been cast in the form of an effective biological half-life. The rate of decrease of radiation exposure is then affected by both the physical and biological half-life, giving an effective half-life for the isotope in the body. Though the biological half-life cannot be expected to be as precise as the physical half-life, it is useful to compute an effective half-life from

$$\frac{1}{T_{Effective}} = \frac{1}{T_{Physical}} + \frac{1}{T_{Biological}}$$

11 If the half-life of an element is 2 days, how much of that element is left after 6 days?

A 1/2

B 1/4

C 1/8

D 1/16

12 Technetium-99m is a widely used radioactive tracer isotope in Nuclear Medicine. It is one of the favorites for diagnostic scans because of short physical and biological half-lives. It clears from the body very quickly after the imaging procedures. ^{99m}Tc has a half-life of approximately 6 hrs. If the effective half-life is 0.2 days, what is the biological half-life of ^{99m}Tc?

A 0.1 days

B 0.2 days

C 1 day

D 2 days

13 Phosporus-32 is often used for bone scans because it tends to be held in bones. The biological half-life of ^{32}P is 257 days. If the half-life outside the body is only 14 days, how much of the element will remain in the body after 53 days 3hrs?

    A 1/2
    B 1/4
    C 1/8
    D 1/16

14 Strontium-90 has an extremely long half-life of 1.1×10^4 days. In the body, it mimics calcium. Which statement about ^{90}Sr is true?

    A ^{90}Sr would be a good element to use in medical imaging because of its long physical half-life

    B ^{90}Sr is particularly dangerous to use in medical imaging because it has a long biological half-life along with a long physical half-life

    C ^{90}Sr would be useful in medical imaging because it has a short biological half-life

    D ^{90}Sr would be useful in medical imaging because it has a short effective half-life

UNIT 5

Questions 15–17

In angelfish, certain genes control whether or not the offspring will develop malignant tumors. This trait is controlled by a specific allele, and the propensity to develop a malignant tumor is considered recessive. If the fish is heterozygous for this trait, it will develop a benign tumor.

15 Two angelfish are mated and the female is homozygous dominant, and the male is heterozygous. 50 offspring are produced. How many of these will develop benign tumors?

    A 50

    B 25

    C 10

    D 0

16 If two parents with benign tumors are mated, and 20 offspring are produced, what will the outcome be?

    A 5 with no tumor, 10 with malignant tumors, and 5 with benign tumors

    B 10 with no tumor, 5 with malignant tumors, and 5 with benign tumors

    C 10 with no tumor, 0 with malignant tumors, and 10 with benign tumors

    D 5 with no tumor, 5 with malignant tumors, and 10 with benign tumors

In addition to the formation of tumors, the color of the angelfish and whether the tail is a fan-tail or not are controlled by separate alleles. A fan-tail is considered a recessive trait, heterozygous results in a normal tail. In the case of color, black and silver are the basic colors, where black is considered recessive. In the case of a heterozygous for black and silver, a silver fish with black stripes is produced.

17 A striped fan-tail angelfish is mated with a black normal-tail angelfish. Which is a possible phenotype?

    A 25% silver with a fan-tail

    B 75% striped with a normal tail

    C 25% black with a fan-tail

    D 33% black with a normal tail

UNIT 6

Questions 18–21

The mucosal surface of the digestive system represents a vast surface covered by a delicate epithelial barrier (IEC) with extensive microvilli (Mv) to increase the surface area. Immune surveillance of mucosal surfaces such as the digestive tract requires the delivery of intact macromolecules and micro-organisms across epithelial barriers to organized mucosal lymphoid tissues. M cells (MC) in the epithelium transport foreign macromolecules and micro-organisms to antigen-presenting cells within and under the epithelial barrier. The M cell transport system is crucial for induction of protective mucosal immune responses and also provides an entry route into the mucosa and thus plays a key role in the pathogenesis of certain bacterial and viral diseases. The M cell pathway also transports non-pathogenic commensal bacteria into organized mucosal lymphoid tissues.

The organization of the lymphoid tissue is composed of Peyer's patches (PP), lamina propria lymphocytes (LPLs) and intraepithelial lymphocytes (IELs). Peyer's patches contain five or more lymphoid follicles and are found predominantly in the terminal ileum. The centre of the follicle consists of B lymphocytes surrounded by mantles of mixed cellularity. The inter-follicular region contains T lymphocytes. Unlike the normal gut epithelial cells, M cells allow ready attachment of luminal particulate antigens (Ag)s to their surfaces. The attachment of Ags and their subsequent endocytosis in pincytotic vesicles (Pv) by M cells appears to operate selectively due to the large amount of dietary Ags that pass through the gut lumen every day. The IELs are situated between the epithelial cells and above the lamina propria. IELs have been shown to exhibit cytolytic and possibly immuno-regulatory functions through the secretion of a variety of cytokines, suggesting an important role in local immuno-surveillance of the IEC and the regional microenvironment. The lamina propria lymphoid tissue exists as a diffuse collection of cells including T lymphocytes, B lymphocytes, plasma cells, macrophages (MØ), mast cells and small numbers of eosinophils and neutrophils. The vast majority of the B cells are IgA producing cells and the remaining are IgM producing cells.

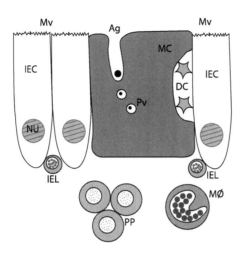

(DC – dendritic cells, Nu - nucleus).

18 What is the structural element shown from the diagram and the passage?

    A Peyer's Patches
    B Intraepithelial lymphocyte
    C Microvilli
    D M Cells

19 What is the function of the antigen receptor in the lymphoid tissue of the digestive system?

    A To help present the antigen to the IEL for the production of immune response system
    B To kill invading microorganisms
    C To aid in the digestion of foreign macromolecules and microorganisms
    D To assist in endocytosis of the antigen and transport to the nucleus

Dendritic cells are bone-marrow-derived antigen presenting cell (APC)s that are found both in lymphoid and non-lymphoid tissues, where they exert a sentinel-like function. They are the most effective APCs and are crucial to the induction of the immune response. In mucosal-associated lymphoid tissues, DCs lie beneath the epithelial M cells and, thus, are ideally placed to capture Ags transported across the mucosal barrier. Dendritic cells express tight junction proteins and penetrate the mucosal barrier to interact with luminal bacterial Ags. Based on functional and phenotypic characteristics, DCs can be classified as immature/inactive and mature/activated.

Immature DCs exist in peripheral tissues including the intestinal mucosa and are equipped for phagocytosis of Ags and bacteria. After taking up Ags and receiving appropriate activation signals they migrate to the paracortical area of the regional mesenteric lymph nodes. During migration they lose their phagocytic capacity and the processed Ag is re-expressed in a stable form at the cell surface for T cell recognition and intimate interaction.

20 How could DCs be involved in persistent infections such as herpes simplex?

    A The infectious agent does not produce an Ag that is recognized by the DC

    B The infectious agent is not recognized by the M cells and therefore cannot be transported to the DC

    C The infectious agent prevents activation and maturation of the DC

    D The infectious agent is toxic to the DC

21 What makes M cells unique from other intestinal epithelial cells?

    A MC are not polarized and therefore do not have an apical and basolateral surface

    B MC can undergo phagocytosis

    C IEC produce mucus which prevents antigens from attaching to their surfaces

    D IEC cannot interact with lymphocytes

UNIT 7

Questions 22–27

The coagulation cascade is a step-by-step process that occurs when a blood vessel is injured. The end result of the coagulation cascade is a blood clot (thrombus) that creates a barrier over the injury site, protecting it until it heals.

The Coagulation Cascade

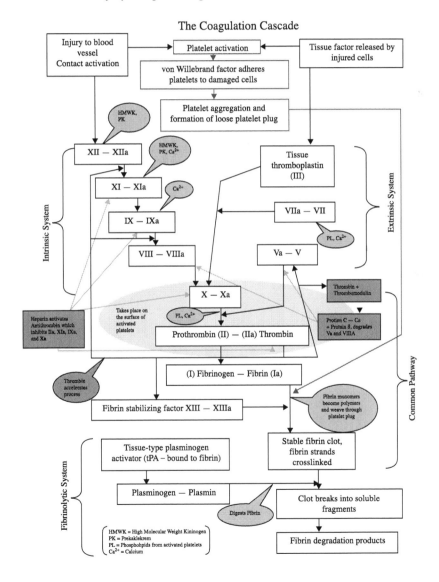

22 Which molecule would be most useful to administer to a patient suffering from a heart attack caused by a thrombus blocking the coronary arteries?

    A Plasminogen
    B Heparin
    C Factor XIII
    D Tissue plasminogen activator

23 Hemophilia A is classic hemophilia (a disease referring to the inability to clot blood). It is an X-linked disorder resulting from a deficiency in factor VIII, a key component of the coagulation cascade. There are severe, moderate and mild forms of hemophilia A that reflect the level of active factor VIII in the plasma. Which section of the coagulation cascade is directly affected by hemophilia A?

    A Extrinsic pathway
    B Intrinsic pathway
    C Common pathway
    D Fibrinolytic system

Tests for Coagulation:

    I.   Partial Thromboplastin Time: PTT is measured by using a citrated sample, which arrests coagulation by binding calcium
    II. Prothrombin Time: PT is the time it takes plasma to clot after addition of tissue factor
    III. Thrombin Time: TCT is the time it takes plasma to clot after the addition of thrombin

24 Which of the above tests would be useful in diagnosing Hemophilia A?

    A I
    B II
    C III
    D None of the above

25 What would be the result of a deficiency in either protein C or protein S?

    A Inability of the blood to clot
    B Increase in the time it takes the blood to clot
    C Thrombotic tendency
    D Inadequate information provided to answer this question

26 Congenital factor XIII deficiency is an extremely rare disorder, with an estimated prevalence of only 1 in 5 million individuals. The disorder is inherited as an autosomal recessive trait, and so females as well as males are affected. How would a deficiency in factor XIII effect blood clotting?

    A It would have no effect on blood clotting because it is not involved in the intrinsic of extrinsic pathway
    B It would cause an increase in the tendency to form thrombosis because fibrinogen cannot be broken down by plasmin
    C It would cause a tendency to bleed due to poor wound healing, and scarring from the clot breakdown at the site of injury
    D It would cause tendency to bleed because it would result in insufficient platelet activation

27 Which coagulation test would be useful in detecting a factor XIII deficiency?

    A I
    B II
    C III
    D None of the above

UNIT 8

Questions 28–29

The basal metabolic rate (BMR) of the human body is the energy expenditure that is required to perform functions such as the beating of the heart, breathing, digestion and growth. The BMR of children is high compared to adults due to the biosynthesis of components for growth. The amount of energy released in body processes depends mainly on the volume V of the tissues while the rate of energy loss depends on the surface area A of the body.

A good estimation of a person's BMR is the Katch-McArdle formula based on lean body mass.

BMR = 370 + (21.6 (LBM)) where LBM stands for Lean Body Mass

28 What would be the units of the surface area to volume ratio?

    A m^2
    B m^{-1}
    C m
    D m^{-2}

29 Given the above information, which of the following statements is true?

    A Children are much more at risk of hypothermia (low temperature) than adults
    B Small people need to eat more relative to their mass than do larger people, everything else being equal.
    C Both a and b
    D Neither a or b

UNIT 9

Questions 30–33

Mitosis is nuclear division plus cytokinesis, and produces two identical daughter cells. The stages of mitosis include prophase, prometaphase, metaphase, anaphase, and telophase. Interphase is often included in discussions of mitosis, but interphase is technically not part of mitosis, but rather encompasses stages G1, S, and G2 of the cell cycle.

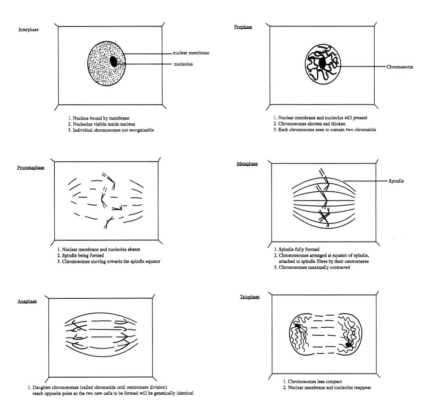

30 At which stage of mitosis would chromosomes be visible in the nucleus?

    A Interphase

    B Prophase

    C Prometaphase

    D Metaphase

31 Cancer is essentially caused by uncontrolled cell growth. An oncologist examines
    three biopsy samples of the same tissue in a microscope. Sample #1 contains 5% of
    its cells in mitosis, sample #2 contains 20% of its cells in mitosis, sample #3 contains
    7% of its cells in mitosis. Which biopsy sample is likely to be cancerous?

    A Sample #1
    B Sample #2
    C Sample #1 and #3
    D None of them are cancerous

Meiosis is a two-part (meiosis I and meiosis II) cell division process in organisms that
sexually reproduce. Through a sequence of steps, the replicated genetic material in a
parent cell is distributed to four daughter cells.

Meiosis I

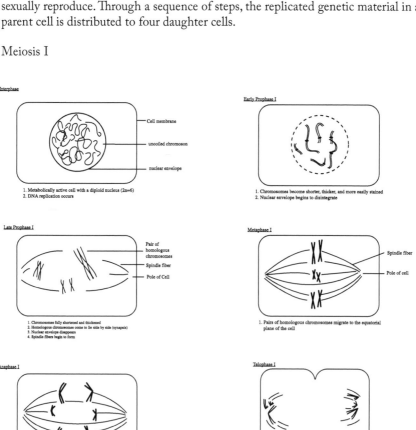

Meiosis II

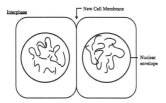

Interphase — New Cell Membrane

Nuclear envelope

1. The chromosomes uncoil and resume the appearance seen in interphase
2. The nuclear envelope reappears, resulting in two haploid nuclei (n=3)
3. First cell division is completed, resulting in two haploid cells

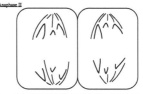

Prophase II

1. Chromosomes become aligned on the equatorial plane
2. Fibres of the spindle are reformed

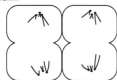

Metaphase II

Pole of cell

Spindle fiber

Equator of cell

1. Chromosomes become aligned on the equatorial plane
2. Fibers of the spindle are reformed

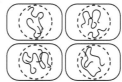

Anaphase II

1. Centromeres divide, separating the chromatids which move to opposite poles as chromosomes

Telophase II

1. Movement of chromosomes to the poles is complete
2. Spindle disappears
3. Cell division starts

Interphase

1. Chromosomes uncoil and resume interphase appearance
2. Nuclear envelope reappears, resulting in four haploid nuclei (n=3)
3. Second cell division completed, resulting in four haploid cells

32 Which statement regarding mitosis and meiosis is incorrect?

A Both processes involve prophase, metaphase, anaphase, and telophase

B The chromosomes line up singly during the metaphases of mitosis and both parts of meiosis

C Both processes involve cytokinesis in the formation of the daughter cells

D Chromosome replication is necessary for both processes

33 Which event does prophase of mitosis and meiosis have in common?

A Nuclear membrane disintegration

B Chromosome migrate toward equatorial center

C Chromosome condensation

D DNA replication

UNIT 10

Questions 34–38

The extracellular matrix (ECM) is a complex structural entity surrounding and supporting cells that are found within mammalian tissues. One particular ECM protein that is involved in a variety of processes including tissue repair, embryogenesis, blood clotting, and cell migration/adhesion is fibronectin (FN). The structure of FN is made of three domains called type I, II and III, the most abundant of which is the type III. Twelve type I modules make up the amino-terminal and carboxy-terminal region of the molecule, only two type II modules are found in the molecule, and depending on the tissue type and/or cellular conditions, 15-17 type III modules are present. Due to the multitude of molecules with which FN can interact, a number of researchers have examined various fragments of FN to determine their exact biological function. Below is a graph of cellular adhesion to different FN domains

Cellular Adhesion to Different FN Domains

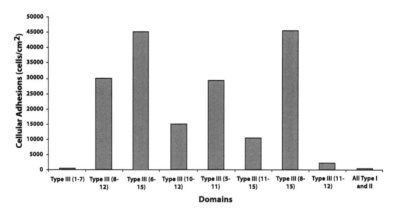

34 Which domains have the least amount of involvement in cell adhesion?

    A   Type I and II

    B   Type III (11-15)

    C   Type III (6-15)

    D   Type III (10-12)

35 Which domains contribute the most to cell adhesion?

 A Type III (6-8)
 B Type III (8-10)
 C Type III (10-12)
 D Type III (12-15)

An assay is performed in which different cell surface integrin receptors are incubated with different FN domain fragments to determine how the different receptors specifically interact with FN. The optical density reading corresponds to number of receptors binding to the fragments.

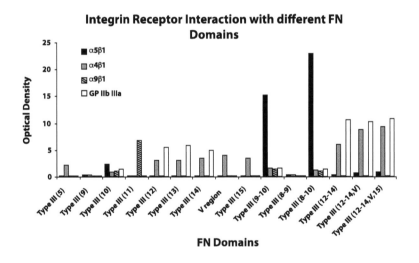

36 Which receptor demonstrates a synergistic effect when binding to multiple domains at the same time?

 A α5β1
 B α4β1
 C α9β1
 D GPIIbIIIa

37 GPIIbIIIa is present on blood platelets and is involved in the formation of a blood clot by connecting platelets via proteins. What effect would a defect in the V region that interfered with the ability of FN to bind to a receptor have on clot formation?

    A It would result in spontaneous clot formation

    B It would result in a reduced ability to form a blood clot and therefore, excessive bleeding could occur

    C It would have no effect on blood clotting

    D There is not enough information provided to determine its effect on clotting

38 What is the most likely reason for the fact that all four receptors have some affinity for the Type III (8-10) domains?

    A The combination of the three domains provides the proper conformation for the receptors to bind

    B There is a common ligand in Type III (10) that is able to bind to the all four receptors

    C There is a common ligand in Type III (9) and in Type III (10) that is able to bind to all four receptors

    D This domain is a larger fragment and thus maintains more of the functionality of the entire FN molecule and therefore is able to bind to all four receptors

UNIT 11

Questions 39–43

The use of levers is to maximize the amount of work done over the work input. One particular aspect of this is the movement of parts of the human body. Muscles pull on tendons connected to bones in order to transfer movement. The three parts of a lever, fulcrum(F), resistance arm(R) and effort arm(E), work together to make it possible to lift a weight using less force or for the same force to produce more movement. Below are the sets of levers possible using these three tools. The human jaw is a precise instrument used in the mastication of food. It is also a lever system. There are three main muscles involved in jaw movement: the masseter, temporalis and lateral pterygoid muscles. Below are the three possible systems of levers. Figure 2 shows a diagram of the muscles of mastication.

Lever Systems

R↓ E↓	R↓ E↑	E↑ R↓
F	F	F
Class I	Class II	Class III

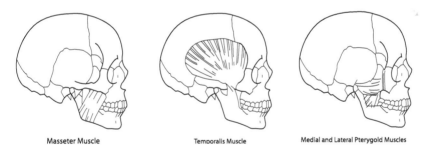

| Masseter Muscle | Temporalis Muscle | Medial and Lateral Pterygoid Muscles |

Figure 1

39 What type of lever system does the jaw represent during the crushing of food?

    A Class I
    B Class II
    C Class III
    D More than one type exists

40 The muscle/s responsible for crushing of food are:

    A Masseter, temporalis and medial pterygoid
    B Masseter only
    C Temporalis only
    D Masseter and temporalis

Figure 2

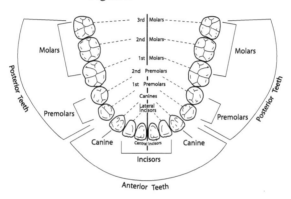

41 In Figure 2, what force is required from the muscles when the anterior teeth use x newtons of force to incise through an apple given that the average distance from the muscles to the fulcrum is 2cm and the incisors are 10cm away.

    A 8 ×
    B 4 ×
    C 5 ×
    D 1/5 ×

42 In Figure 2, which teeth are the most likely to fracture during the chewing of food?

    A Premolar teeth
    B Molar teeth
    C Incisors
    D All teeth equally

43 The posterior teeth of the human dentition are designed to crush food with 4
times more force than the anterior teeth. Given that the incisors lie exactly in the
centre of the grouping of anterior teeth. What is the approximate distance from
the posterior teeth to the anterior teeth if the molar teeth are 4cm away from the
fulcrum-temporomandibular joint?

   A 7.5cm
   B 5.5cm
   C 6.5cm
   D 8.5cm

UNIT 12

Questions 44–45

When a person consumes a drug, the level of distribution throughout the body and excretion can be estimated. The *apparent volume* (V_D) into which a drug is distributed can be measured by the equation $V_D = d/C_0$ where d is the dosage of the drug and C_0 is the initial plasma concentration. The following estimates apply

$V_D < 5$ $\Rightarrow$ drug is retained within the vascular tissues

$V_D < 15$ $\Rightarrow$ drug is restricted to the extracellular fluid

$V_D \geq 15$ $\Rightarrow$ drug is distributed to the entire body

V_D is in liters (L)

44 Morphine is an opioid drug used in the control of severe pain. Assuming no contraindications for use, what would be the minimum dose of morphine needed to suppress the pain a patient is experiencing pain after a major car accident with injuries to multiple body parts when an initial plasma concentration of 6.7×10^{-3}mg/L is required?

     A 1.0×10^2mg

     B 1.0×10^1 mg

     C 1.0×10^{-1}mg

     D 1.0×10^{-2} mg

45 The "plasma clearance rate" of a drug is the volume of blood or plasma cleared of a drug in unit time. It is given by the equation $Cl_p = V_D K_{el}$ where K_{el} is the rate of elimination. $K_{el} = 0.69/t_{1/2}$ where $t_{1/2}$ is the half-live of the drug. Given that the half-life of morphine is 2 hours, what is the clearance rate of the drug?

     A 4.3×10^1 Lh^{-1}

     B 8.6×10^{-2} Lh^{-1}

     C 5.2 Lh^{-1}

     D 2.6×10^3 Lh^{-1}

UNIT 13

Questions 46–48

Pythons have adapted to the lifestyle of eating large infrequent meals by altering their physiological response after feeding. These adaptations have resulted in changes in the metabolic rate (SDA), alterations in organ growth and nutrient transport, and modifications in ventilation and cardiovascular activity. The metabolic rate is measured by the volume of oxygen consumption. Within hours of swallowing prey, the python's metabolic rate begins to rise. The metabolic rate peaks at a rate of about 20 times the rate during fasting and then slowly decreases to fasting levels as seen in the graph below. As meal size increases, so does the magnitude of the metabolic response.

Changes in Oxygen Consumption after Feeding

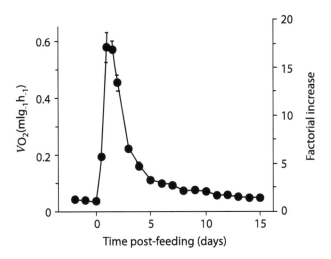

Changes in Ventilation, Heart Rate, and Blood Flow after Feeding

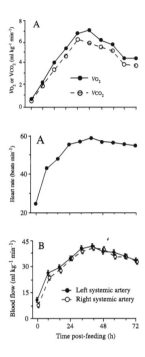

Both the ventilation system and cardiovascular system change in response to the increases in metabolic rate. The above graphs show changes in ventilation (CO_2 and O_2), heart rate, and blood flow following a feeding.

46 Approximately how long does the metabolic rate remain elevated after a feeding?

    A 3 hrs
    B ~1-2 days
    C ~3-5 days
    D ~6-14 days

47 What is the average blood flow three days after feeding?

    A 45 ml kg^{-1} min^{-1}
    B 10 ml kg^{-1} min^{-1}
    C 30 ml kg^{-1} min^{-1}
    D 20 ml kg^{-1} min^{-1}

48 What advantage does the python gain from having the ventilation rate, heart rate, and blood volume all peak at about 48 hrs post feeding?

    A The metabolic rate peaks at about 2 days post feeding due to the increase in oxygen levels resulting from peaks in ventilation, heart rate, and blood volume

    B The metabolic rate peeks at about 5 days post feeding following the increase in oxygen levels resulting from peaks in ventilation, heart rate, and blood volume

    C The metabolic rate would not be affected by the increase in oxygen levels resulting from peaks in ventilation, heart rate, and blood volume

    D The metabolic rate remains elevated for a longer period of time due to the increase in oxygen levels resulting from peaks in ventilation, heart rate, and blood volume

UNIT 14

Questions 49–51

Local anesthetics (LA) are drugs used to prevent pain by causing a reversible block of nerve conduction. They are weak bases that exist mainly in a protonated form (BH⁺ in diagram) at body pH. As shown in the diagram, the LA molecules penetrate the nerve in a non-ionized form and once inside the axon, some ionized molecules are formed which block the nerve transmission.

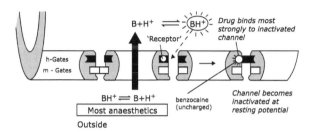

49   Dental abscesses cause severe pain to a patient. They are acidic in nature. What effect would this have on the efficacy of benozocaine (a type of local anesthetic)?

    A   Enhance the effectiveness of the local anesthesia

    B   Decrease the effectiveness of the local anesthesia

    C   Have no effect on the local anesthetic administration

    D   Need more information

50   Local anesthetics contain a small amount of adrenaline. Very rarely when a dentist gives an "inferior alveolar nerve block", anesthetizing the lower jaw, the needle can penetrate the maxillary artery which supplies part of the eye and deposit the LA into the artery. What visual disturbances could be caused?

    A   Blurring of near objects

    B   Sharpness of near objects

    C   No disturbances

    D   Temporary blindness

51   If a 2m tall person steps in a sharp object and he feels the pain only 1 sec later, what is the average speed of the nerve transmission in the pain fibers?

    A $2.0 \times 10 \text{ cms}^{-1}$

    B $1.0 \times 10^2 \text{ cms}^{-1}$

    C $1.0 \times 10 \text{ cms}^{-1}$

    D $2.0 \times 10^2 \text{ cms}^{-1}$

UNIT 15

Questions 52–56

Enzymes act as biological catalysts that help speed up reactions by lowering the activation energy needed to bring reactants to their "transition state." In this unstable condition, bonds break and the reaction proceed. The reaction itself is often described by the following;

$$E + S \rightarrow ES \rightarrow P + E$$

E = Enzyme   ES = Enzyme-Substrate Complex
S = Substrate (s)   P = Products (s)

Enzymes can carry out their catalytic functions only with particular substrates and only under particular environmental conditions. This characteristic of enzymes is referred to as enzyme specificity. The enzyme specificity in four different enzymes is shown in the figure below

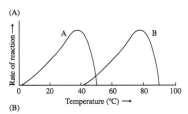

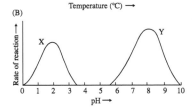

52 At 35°C the rate of the reaction catalysed by enzyme A begins to level off. Which statement best explains this observation?

   A The temperature is too far below optimum
   B The enzyme has become saturated with substrate
   C Both A and B
   D Neither A nor B

53 Which statement regarding enzymes X and Y is true?

  A They could not possible be at work in the same part of the body at the same time

  B They have different temperature ranges at which they work best

  C At pH 4.5, enzyme Y works faster than enzyme X

  D At their appropriate pH ranges, both enzymes work at the same rate

54 An enzyme-substrate complex can form when the substrate(s) bind(s) to an active site of the enzyme. Which condition could change the conformation of an enzyme such that its substrate is unable to bind to it?

  A Enzyme A at 40°C

  B Enzyme B at pH 2

  C Enzyme X at pH 4

  D Enzyme Y at 37°C

55 Which of the following would prevent digestive enzyme Y from bringing its substrate to the transition state?

  A Any temperature below optimum

  B Any pH where the rate of reaction is not at a maximum

  C Any pH lower than 5.5

  D Any temperature higher than 37°C

56 Enzymes X and Y are both protein digesting enzymes found in humans. Where would they most likely be found?

  A X in mouth; Y in small intestine

  B X in small intestine; Y in mouth

  C X in stomach; Y in small intestine

  D X in stomach; Y in mouth

UNIT 16

Questions 57-60

The immune response is part of the body's "specific defense system." Two aspects of this defense mechanism are the primary and secondary immune responses. When the body is first exposed to a foreign antigen (primary immune response), B-lymphocytes or B-cells, as well as macrophages, come in contact with the antigen. When the macrophages digest the antigen-bearing agent and display the antigen on their surface, T-helper cells (one kind of T-cell) become activated. The T-helper cells assist other types of T-cells in responding to the agent and interact with B-cells, causing some of them to differentiate into antibody-secreting plasma cells. Such humoral antibodies (immuno-globulins) can be produced and released by plasma cells for many weeks as other effector components of the immune system help destroy the invading organisms. During this time, the host suffers through various symptoms (depending on the invader), but in addition, sensitized memory cells are produced that can remain dormant for decades. Upon second exposure to the same antigen, the memory cells (various T-cells and B-cells) can give rise to clones of appropriate effector cells much more rapidly than the first time; this is a secondary immune response.

The figure below characterizes both primary and secondary responses.

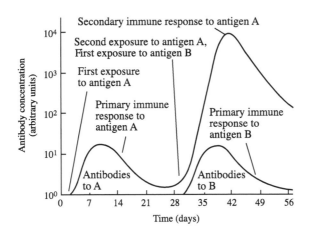

57 The HIV virus can infect T-helper cells, preventing then from functioning properly and often killing them. Which aspect/aspects of the body's defense is/are affected by the virus?

    A Primary immune response
    B Secondary immune response
    C Both A and B
    D Neither A nor B

58 Approximately when would the secondary response peak in response to antigen B?

    A 40
    B 42
    C 56
    D 70

59 What could be the result of administration of ampicillin to a patient where it is discovered during initial treatment has a serious allergy to the drug?

    A When the drug is administered a second time, the patient's allergic response is more severe
    B When the drug is administered a second time, the patient should be able to receive the benefits of the drug faster
    C When the drug is administered a second time, the patients allergic response is similar to the initial reaction to the drug
    D Both B and C

60 Approximately how many more antibodies are produced during the secondary immune response compared to the primary immune response?

    A ~ 10 ×'s as many
    B ~ 100 ×'s as many
    C ~ 1000 ×'s as many
    D ~ 10,000 ×'s as many

UNIT 17

Questions 61–64

A set of experiments was performed to examine the effects of ultraviolet radiation (UV) on the bacterium E. coli. It is known that purines and pyrimidines absorb UV radiation at 260 nanometers (nm). Fewer colonies suggest that cells have died, while smaller colonies suggest that growth has been inhibited.

Experiment 1

The undersides of two glass petri dishes (A and B) were divided in half (each dish divided into sides 1 and 2) using a marking pencil. Melted agar and nutrients were poured into the dishes and allowed to harden. A sample of bacterial culture was streaked across the entire surface of each dish before covering with the glass lid. Treatment was as follows: With the lid removed, dish A was radiated with UV (260 nm) on side 1 only, while dish B was radiated with green light (550 nm) on side 1 only. Both dishes were then covered and incubated in a dark container.

Experiment 2

The procedures used in Experiment 1 were repeated except that the dishes were then exposed to regular incandescent light for 20 minutes before being incubated in a dark container. The results of both experiments are summarized in the table below.

Number and Characteristics of Bacterial Colonies			
Dish A		Dish B	
Side 1	Side 2	Side 3	Side 4
Experiment 1			
5 large	30 large	31 large	29 large
5 small			
Experiment 2			
10 large	29 large	30 large	31 large
10 small			

61 Which statement is true concerning the colonies in experiment 1?

    A 25% of the colonies exposed to UV light show the effects of radiation

    B Exposure to UV light results in 1/3 the number of colonies that result in bacteria not exposed to UV light

    C 2/3 of the colonies on the plate were not affected by UV exposure

    D UV exposure results in 1/8 of the cells dying

62 Which statement is a reasonable interpretation of the results obtained by comparing dish A from both experiments?

    A UV exposure does ½ the damage of incandescent light

    B Incandescent light exposure helps magnify the effects of UV damage

    C Incandescent light exposure helps repair the effects of UV damage

    D UV exposure does twice as much damage as incandescent light exposure

63 Experiment 1 was repeated, however, the glass lid was not removed prior to UV radiation. The new results were as follows: After incubation, side 1 of dish A had 29 large colonies and side 2 had 30 large colonies. How can this result be interpreted?

    A Glass effectively blocks the effects of UV radiation

    B UV radiation can inhibit growth, but does not kill

    C Glass has no effect on bacterial colony formation

    D UV radiation has no effect on bacterial colony formation

64 What is/are the controls for these experiments?

    A Side 2 of dish A

    B Side 1 of dish B

    C Side 1 of both dish A and B

    D Side 2 of both dish A and B

UNIT 18

Questions 65-69

The inheritance of traits was first demonstrated by Joseph Mendel, who discovered many of the fundamentals of genetics. Mendel studied the inheritance of traits in pea plants, looking at such traits as plant height, seed color, and seed texture. Mendel discovered that for each of these traits, there exist two distinct physical characteristics, or phenotypes. His studies of inheritance patterns led him to the conclusion that each of the traits was coded for by a gene with two different forms or alleles, one for each character, such as T for tall and t for short, Y for yellow and y for green, and R for round and r for wrinkled. Also, each individual had two copies of the gene for any trait, one from each parent; this two-allele set was called the genotype. Any homozygous individual, with two identical alleles for a trait, expressed the phenotype that corresponded to that allele. Heterozygous individuals, with different alleles, would express the phenotype of the dominant allele, the first of each set listed, over those of the recessive alleles, listed second. Finally, Mendel discovered that each parent randomly passes on one of his/her two alleles to each offspring, and that the laws of statistics could be used to describe possible offspring using structures known as Punnett squares.

	G	g
G	GG	Gg
g	Gg	gg

65. What is the probability of two heterozygous tall pea plants having a heterozygous tall offspring?

   A. 25%
   B. 50%
   C. 75%
   D. 100%

66. Which of the following genotypes would yield a tall plant with wrinkled yellow peas?

    A. ttYyRR
    B. TtYyRr
    C. TtYYrr
    D. TTyyrr

67. What is the theoretical phenotypic ratio for the offspring of two pea plants that are heterozygous for both height and color?

    A. 3:1
    B. 1:2:1
    C. 9:3:3:1
    D. 6:4:4:2

68. A pea plant with the genotype ttYyRr would have what phenotype?

    A. short, yellow, round
    B. short, yellow, wrinkled
    C. short, green, round
    D. tall, yellow, round

69. Which of the following pea plant crosses is most likely to yield a plant that is heterozygous for height, color, and smoothness?

    A. TtRRYy x TTRryy
    B. TtrrYy x TtRRYY
    C. TTRryy x ttRrYY
    D. TTrrYY x ttRRyy

UNIT 19

Questions 70-74

Genetic diseases are conditions caused by abnormalities in genes or chromosomes. The term genetic disease generally refers to inherited conditions present in an individual's genetic code, as opposed to disorders caused by acquired abnormalities such as cancer. Diseases caused by defective genes can be inherited on the non-sex chromosomes, or autosomes, in the typical Mendelian fashion of dominant/recessive pairs. Genetic disease can also be sex-linked, where the gene in question is inherited on the chromosome, making men much more susceptible to the disease, as they lack a second X chromosome to mask the recessive effect. Sex linkage is generally characterized by a predominance of the disease among men, with women generally being unafflicted or carriers. One way of representing the inheritance of genetic disease is through family trees, in which squares represent men, circles represent women, horizontal connections indicate marriage, and vertical connections indicate children.

70. In the karyotype below, which shows the chromosomes of a child with Down Syndrome, which chromosome is responsible for the disorder?

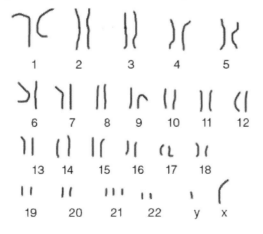

A. 6
B. 9
C. 21
D. Y

71. What is the mode of inheritance for Tay-Sachs disease, the disease examined in the family tree below?

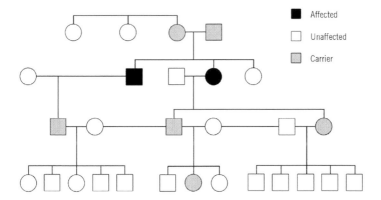

A. sex-linked dominant

B. sex-linked recessive

C. autosomal dominant

D. autosomal recessive

72. Huntington's disease is a debilitating genetic neurological disorder that typically does not present with symptoms until late middle age, which means that many afflicted individuals have children before diagnosis. Any child of a parent with Huntington's disease has at least a 50% chance of inheriting the disease, with the probability increasing depending on the specific genotypes of each parent. From this information, what is the mode of inheritance of Huntington's disease?

A. sex-linked dominant

B. sex-linked recessive

C. autosomal dominant

D. autosomal recessive

73. Hemophilia is an X-linked recessive disorder that inhibits the body's ability to form blood clots. What is the probability that the children of a carrier woman and an afflicted man will have hemophilia?

A. 0% for females, 50% for males

B. 50% for females, 50% for males

C. 50% for females, 100% for males

D. 100% for females, 100% for males

74. A disorder that afflicts members of a particular family is known to be genetic, and affects both male and female children, but is only passed on by the females. What is the most likely source of the genetic defect?

    A. nuclear DNA
    B. ribosomal RNA
    C. nuclear RNA
    D. mitochondrial DNA

UNIT 20

Questions 75-79

Deoxyribonucleic acid, or DNA, is the molecule that carries the genetic code for an organism. DNA is composed of strands of nitrogenous bases that are bonded together by phosphate bonds between sugar groups. The bases, guanine (G), cytosine (C), adenine (A), and thymine (T), are read in the genetic code from the 5' end of the chain to the 3' end. In normal, inert DNA, strands are bound together into a winding double helix by hydrogen bonds between complementary bases. G pairs with C, A pairs with T, and the two chains are bound in opposite 5'-3' orientations. DNA is duplicated by unwinding two strands and forming a new DNA complement for each one. Ribonucleic acid, the molecule that carries the genetic code to the cell's machinery, is identical to DNA except that it contains uracil (U) in place of thymine and generally exists in single strands transcribed in reverse 5'-3' orientation from DNA.

75. What is the DNA complement of the DNA string 5'–GAATCGGCTTAC–3'?

   A. 5'–CTTAGCCGAATG–3'
   B. 5'–GTAAGCCGATTC–3'
   C. 5'–CUUAGCCGAAUG–3'
   D. 5'–GUAAGCCGAUUC–3'

76. What would be the sequence of the RNA strand transcribed from the complement of the DNA strand 5'–ATCGCTAGCCTAGTAG–3'?

   A. 5'–TAGCGATCGGATCATG–3'
   B. 5'–CTACTAGGCTAGCGAT–3'
   C. 5'–UAGCGAUCGGAUCAUG–3'
   D. 5'–CUACUAGGCUAGCGAU–3'

77. If 20% of the bases in a sample of double-stranded DNA are guanine, how many are thymine?

    A. 60%
    B. 40%
    C. 30%
    D. 20%

78. Besides hydrogen, which elements are involved in the hydrogen bonding that holds two DNA strands together in the double helix?

    A. oxygen and nitrogen
    B. oxygen and carbon
    C. carbon and phosphorus
    D. phosphorus and nitrogen

79. A sample of nucleic acid is composed of 21% guanine, 26% adenine, 23% cytosine, and 30% uracil. What kind of nucleic acid is the sample?

    A. single-stranded DNA
    B. double-stranded DNA
    C. single-stranded RNA
    D. double-stranded RNA

UNIT 21

Questions 80-84

Calcitonin and parathyroid hormone, or PTH, are the two hormones that regulate the levels of calcium in the blood. When calcium levels in the blood stray outside the acceptable range, either the thyroid gland produces calcitonin or the parathyroid gland produces PTH. Calcitonin stimulates calcium deposit in the bones, taking calcium up from the blood and binding it in bone mass, while PTH stimulates bone resorption, breaking down bone to release calcium into the bloodstream. Working together, the two hormones keep the levels of calcium in the blood in the range necessary to support proper physiological function in the body.

80. Which of the following physiological functions is most dependent on calcium?

    A. digestion
    B. reproduction
    C. muscle contraction
    D. nerve conduction

81. What change in bone mass would most likely result from a hormone-secreting tumor in the parathyroid gland?

    A. increased bone mass due to lowered PTH levels
    B. increased bone mass due to elevated calcitonin levels
    C. decreased bone mass due to elevated PTH levels
    D. decreased bone mass due to lowered calcitonin levels

82. How would the active levels of PTH and calcitonin change in response to hypocalcemia?

    A. increased calcitonin, increased PTH
    B. increased calcitonin, decreased PTH
    C. decreased calcitonin, decreased PTH
    D. decreased calcitonin, increased PTH

83. Which of the following cells is stimulated by calcitonin?

    A. osteoblast

    B. osteoclast

    C. osteocyte

    D. osteoprogenitor

84. In addition to the skeletal system, which systems are most closely tied to the function of calcitonin and PTH?

    A. nervous and integumentary

    B. lymphatic and respiratory

    C. endocrine and circulatory

    D. reproductive and digestive

UNIT 22

Questions 85–89

The diagram below shows a generalized picture of the four-chambered human heart and the flow of blood to, through, and from it. The diagram is shown from an anterior vantage point, with the anatomical right on the left side of the diagram. Blood returning to the heart from the body and liver or the lungs first enters an atrium from a vein and is then pumped into a ventricle, from where it is pumped back out to the body or pulmonary circuit through an artery.

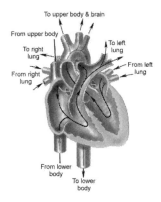

85. In which order does blood flow through the chambers of the heart after returning from the lungs?

    A. right atrium, right ventricle, left atrium, left ventricle
    B. left ventricle, right ventricle, right atrium, left atrium
    C. left atrium, left ventricle, right atrium, right ventricle
    D. right ventricle, left atrium, left ventricle, right atrium

86. Which of the following statements about the heart and circulatory system is false?

    A. Arteries carry oxygenated blood, and veins carry deoxygenated blood.
    B. The left ventricle has the thickest walls in the heart.
    C. The sound of a heat beating is made by the opening and closing of valves.
    D. The heart is regulated by the autonomic nervous system.

87. Which of the following blood vessels is directly connected to the right atrium?

    A. aorta
    B. vena cava
    C. pulmonary artery
    D. pulmonary vein

88. Blood pressure is the highest in which of the chambers of the heart?

    A. right atrium
    B. right ventricle
    C. left atrium
    D. left ventricle

89. During pregnancy, the blood of the fetus is cleaned by the mother. Which of the following structures of the fetal circulatory system is responsible for allowing blood to bypass the liver during pregnancy?

    A. foramen ovale
    B. ductus venosus
    C. placenta
    D. ductus arteriosus

UNIT 23

Questions 90–94

Population ecology is the field of biology that deals with population dynamics and the interactions of species populations with each other and the environment. Interactions with other species and environmental factors both affect populations in drastic ways. Within the boundaries set by these limiting factors, population growth can occur in several different ways. Reproduction is the primary means of growth, but movement in and out of a population also affect its size and growth rate. Ecologists differentiate population size from effective population size, defining effective population size as the number of breeding individuals of an ideal population that would achieve the same genetic reproductive distribution as the population in question. This level of genetic allele distribution can be quantified using the Hardy-Weinberg equations $p + q = 1$ and $p^2 + 2pq + q^2 = 1$. In other words, the frequencies of alleles p and q in a population must total 1, as must the frequencies of the genotypes $pp, pq, qp,$ and qq. In a population with a sex ratio that is not the reproductively optimal 1:1, the effective population size N_e can be calculated using the formula $N_e = {(4 \times M \times F)}/{(M + F)}$, where M and F are the numbers of male and female individuals.

90. What type of population growth is modeled in the diagram below?

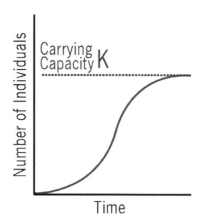

A. exponential
B. linear
C. logistic
D. irruptive

91. Which of the following expressions correctly describes population change as a function of final population (N), initial population (N_0), emigration (E), immigration (I), births (B), and deaths (D)?

A. $N = N_0 - B + D - E + I$
B. $N = N_0 + B - D + E - I$
C. $N = N_0 - B + D - I + E$
D. $N = N_0 + B - D + I - E$

92. The relationship between ants and aphids, in which both species benefit from their interaction, is an example of what type of species interaction?

A. mutualism
B. amensalism
C. commensalism
D. antagonism

93. A certain genetic disorder is caused by a gene on chromosome 6 and affects only the 4% of the population that is homozygous recessive for the defect. Assuming it is an ideal Hardy-Weinberg population, how much of the population is carrying the disease?

A. 16%
B. 20%
C. 32%
D. 40%

94. If there are 30 males in a population of 100 individuals, what is the effective population size?

A. 96
B. 84
C. 64
D. 36

GENERAL CHEMISTRY: **Unit 1**

Questions 1–4

The spontaneity of a reaction involves two variables, enthalpy and entropy. Enthalpy (H) is defined as the amount of heat absorbed by a system at constant pressure. Entropy (S) is a measure of the amount of disorder or randomness in a system. The relationship between reaction spontaneity, entropy and enthalpy is given by the Gibbs free energy function:

$$\Delta G = \Delta H - T\,\Delta S$$

The change in the free energy of a system under standard state conditions is called the standard state free energy of reaction ($\Delta G°$)

$$\Delta G° = \Delta H° - T\Delta S°$$

The balance between the two driving forces that determine whether a reaction is spontaneous (enthalpy and entropy), provides the change in free energy. Enthalpy and entropy terms have different sign conventions.

Favourable	Unfavourable
$\Delta H° < 0$	$\Delta H° > 0$
$\Delta S° > 0$	$\Delta S° < 0$

1. If $\Delta G° < 0$ then,
   - A. The reaction is not spontaneous
   - B. The reaction is spontaneous
   - C. The entropy must be positive
   - D. The enthalpy must be positive

2. Given the following system: $\Delta H = 200$ kJ/mol and $\Delta S = 800$ J/(mol-K). If the temperature of this system increases, what will be the effect on the free energy of the system?
   - A. As the temperature increases, the free energy will become more spontaneous
   - B. As the temperature increases, the free energy will become less spontaneous
   - C. As the temperature increases, the free energy will approach equilibrium
   - D. An increase in temperature will have no effect in the free energy of the system

3. Given the following reaction:

$$2Hg\ (l) + O_2\ (g) \rightarrow 2HgO\ (s)$$

$\Delta H°$ (kJ mol⁻¹)	0	0	-90.79
$\Delta S°$ (J mol⁻¹ K⁻¹)	76.027	205.0	70.7
Substance	Hg (l)	O_2 (g)	HgO (s)

Calculate the free energy of the reaction at 25°C
   A. -117.3 kJ
   B. 64083.3 kJ
   C. 245.3 kJ
   D. -245.3 kJ

4. Entropy can be defined as disorder within a system. $\Delta S = \Delta S$ (products) - ΔS (reactants), so an increase in disorder would result in a positive entropy change. For which of the following processes would ΔS NOT be positive?
   A. A reaction where a molecule is split into two molecules
   B. A reaction where there is an increase in the moles of gas
   C. The boiling of water to water vapour
   D. The freezing of water to ice

UNIT 2

Question 5-8

The relationship between reaction spontaneity, entropy and enthalpy is given by the Gibbs free energy function:

$$\Delta G = \Delta H - T \, \Delta S$$

A negative ΔG indicates a spontaneous reaction.

Sign of ΔG	Sign of ΔH	Sign of ΔS
A	-	+
B	+	-
C	+	+
D	-	-

5. Consider the following table, for which of the choices would the reaction always be spontaneous?
   - A. B
   - B. A
   - C. D
   - D. C

6. Which choice would be spontaneous ONLY at high T?
   - A. C
   - B. A
   - C. D
   - D. B

7. Given a particular reaction where $\Delta H = -181.57$ kJ/mol and $\Delta S = 200$ J/mol·K. If the reaction is performed under NTP conditions, what would be the free energy of the reaction?
   - A. – 121.57 kJ
   - B. -240.17 kJ
   - C. – 59782 kJ
   - D. 59418 kJ

8. Given a negative enthalpy and negative entropy, how would T affect ΔG?

    A. ΔG would be non-spontaneous at all T

    B. ΔG would be spontaneous at all T

    C. ΔG would be non-sponaneous at high T and spontaneous at low T

    D. ΔG would be non-sponaneous at low T and spontaneous at high T

UNIT 3

Questions 9-11

The Downs cell is an industrial electrolytic cell that produces metallic sodium metal from molten Sodium Chloride. Chlorine gas is a by-product of this process. A variety of other very reactive metals are prepared from molten Chloride salts, including Lithium, Magnesium, and Calcium. The first commercial preparation of Sodium metal was performed by Sir Humphrey Davy who used molten NaOH and prepared Oxygen gas as a by-product.

$Na^+(aq) + e^-$	$\rightarrow$	$Na\ (s)\ \ E°= -2.71\ V$
$Mg^{+2}(aq) + 2e^-$	$\rightarrow$	$Mg\ (s)\ \ E°= -2.37\ V$
$Al^{+3}(aq) + 3e^-$	$\rightarrow$	$Al\ (s)\ \ E°= -1.66\ V$
$2H^+(aq) + 2e^-$	$\rightarrow$	$H_2\ (g)\ \ E°= 0.00\ V$
$2H_2O\ (l) + 2e^-$	$\rightarrow$	$H_2\ (g) + OH^-\ (aq)\ E°= -0.83\ V$
$Cl_2\ (g) + 2e^-$	$\rightarrow$	$2Cl^-\ \ E° = 1.36\ V$

9. Which of the following metals can be obtained from an aqueous solution; Al, Mg, or Na?

    A. Al and Mg

    B. Na only

    C. Al only

    D. None can be obtained from an aqueous solution

10. In the Down's cell that is used in the commercial production of Na, which of the following reactions represent what is occurring at the anode?

    A. $2Na^+ + e^- \rightarrow 2Na\ (l)$

    B. $2Na\ (l)\ \ \rightarrow\ \ 2Na^+ + e^-$

    C. $2Cl \rightarrow Cl_2\ (g) + 2e^-$

    D. $Cl_2\ (g) + 2e^- \rightarrow 2Cl^-$

11. What EMF is required to drive the electrolysis of molten NaCl?

    A. 1.35 V

    B. -1.35 V

    C. 4.07 V

    D. -4.07 V

UNIT 4

Questions 12–14

Faraday's law states that the amount of substance produced at an electrode during electrolysis is directly proportional to the amount of current passed through the solution. The proportionality constant is the gram equivalent weight of the substance. Note that:

1 Coulomb = 1 amp-s;

1 Faraday = 96500 coulombs = 1 mole of e⁻

12. How many grams of aluminium are produced if 31500 C is passed through an aluminium nitrate solution (mw_{Al} = 27)?

   A. 27.6 g
   B. 26.4 g
   C. 8.7 g
   D. 2.9 g

13. During the production of molten Li (s) from molten LiCl, 10g of Li are deposited at the cathode after 40 minutes. How many amps were passed through the solution to produce this amount of Li (mw_{Li} = 6.9)?

   A. 117 amp
   B. 0.0012 amp
   C. 58.3 amp
   D. 6993 amp

14. During this same process how many grams of Cl_2 (g) are formed (mw_{Cl} = 35.5)

   A. 0g
   B. 0.86g
   C. 51.4g
   D. 102.8g

UNIT 5

Questions 15-20

Two laws of physics greatly affect divers. *Henry's law* states that the amount of gas dissolving into a liquid (such as blood or tissue), is directly related to the partial pressure of that gas. Recall that the partial pressure of a gas is equal to the amount of that gas in the mixture multiplied by the pressure. In addition, *Boyle's law* states that the gas volume is inversely proportional to the pressure. Therefore, as the gas pressure increases during immersion, the amount of gas entering the blood and tissues increases. Compressed air, which divers breathe, is made up of 21% oxygen and 79% nitrogen; however different gas mixtures have been developed in attempts to prevent some of the complications associated with breathing compressed air at depths for long periods of time. For every 10 meters of depth, the pressure will increase by 1 atm.

15. A scuba diver has a tank filled with 300 L of air, how many L of air will that diver have to breathe at 30 meters depth?

    A. 60 L

    B. 75 L

    C. 100 L

    D. 300 L

16. At a depth of 22 meters, what will be the partial pressures of oxygen and nitrogen respectively, which the diver is breathing?

    A. 0.67; 2.53

    B. 0.21; 0.79

    C. 0.46; 1.74

    D. 0.88; 3.3

17. Nitrogen narcosis, also known as rapture of the deep, is a condition which can occur when the partial pressure of nitrogen rises above a certain level that results in impaired judgement, loss of coordination, and loss of decision making ability. It is sometimes referred to as the "martini effect" since the diver may appear drunk. Divers can experience narcosis at partial pressures of nitrogen as little as 2.2 atm, however it usually doesn't manifest itself until partial pressure closer to 2.7 atm. At what depth could a diver begin to experience nitrogen narcosis?

    A. 24 m

    B. 30 m

    C. 18 m

    D. 12 m

18. Decompression sickness (DCS), or "the bends," is a result of nitrogen gas dissolving out of the blood stream or tissues too quickly thereby forming bubbles. This occurs because the partial pressure acting on the blood or tissue increases with increasing pressure, and then decreases too quickly to continue to hold the gas in solution if the ascent is too fast, so it rapidly comes out of solution. It is similar to what happens when a carbonated beverage container is opened and CO_2 bubbles form in the liquid. Deep sea divers sometimes wear armoured suits which are highly effective in preventing DCS. How do these special suits prevent DCS?
    A. The nitrogen is more easily exhaled within the suit and therefore, the diver doesn't absorb as much nitrogen
    B. The suit prevents compression of the air which is being breathed by the diver, so its as if the diver is simply breathing air at atmospheric pressure and therefore, no extra nitrogen is being absorbed
    C. The exhaled air is vented to the surrounding water, so the diver does not absorb as much nitrogen
    D. The suit allows for better air circulation, so therefore, the diver absorbs less nitrogen

19. Oxygen toxicity can become a serious complication when diving. Oxygen toxicity starts to become a problem when oxygen is breathed at partial pressures above 1.4 atm. What is the maximum depth a diver can dive while breathing compressed air before they may start to encounter oxygen toxicity?
    A. 47 m
    B. 67 m
    C. 27 m
    D. 57 m

20. Special mixtures of gases are sometimes used while diving. One such mixture is called heliox and is a mixture of helium and oxygen, and another is called trimix and usually consists of helium, oxygen, and nitrogen. Which of the following would be an advantage for a commercial diver using 10% oxygen, 50% helium, 40% nitrogen trimix?

    i.   Ability to dive deeper
    ii. No chance of getting DCS
    iii. Less chance of nitrogen narcosis
    iv. Less air consumption

    A. ii and iii
    B. i, iii, and iv
    C. i and iii
    D. All of the above

UNIT 6

Questions 21-22

The ideal gas law, which predicts the behaviour of a gas, states that the pressure of a gas multiplied by the volume of that gas is equal to the moles of the gas multiplied by the gas constant multiplied by the temperature, or more simply

$$PV = nRT$$

In order for a gas to obey the ideal gas equation, three assumptions must be made:

1. Molecules are perfectly elastic (no STICKINESS)
2. Molecules are point masses (no SIZE)
3. Molecules move at random

At high pressure, the intermolecular distances become too short making attractive forces significant. At low temperatures, gases condense meaning that the molecule must stick to one another. Moreover, the liquid has measurable molar volume, and this volume is simply the size of the close-packed molecules of the liquid. Therefore, under these conditions, the gas behaviour deviated significantly from the ideal gas equation. For stickiness to be a factor, the two gas molecules must have a collision. The probability of a collision is the probability of two molecules being in the same place at the same time. The probability of the first molecule being at the place of the collision is proportional to the number density **(n/V)**. The probability of the second one being in the same place is the same, **(n/V)**. Thus the reduction in pressure due to stickiness should be proportional to **(n/V)²**. If the proportionality constant is called **a**, then the ideal pressure is

$$P_{ideal} = P_{real} + a\left(\frac{n^2}{V^2}\right)$$

To correct for the effect of finite molecular volume, we must recognize that in the ideal gas equation the volume used is the "free volume" that the molecules find themselves in. The free volume is just the real (container) volume minus the volume that is taken up by the molecules of the gas itself.

$$V_{Ideal} = V_{real} - nb$$

where **b** is a constant representing the volume of a mole of gas molecules at rest.

21. Van der Waal used the concepts of increased stickiness and decreased volume to come up with the famous Van der Waals equation for real gases. Which of the following represents the Van de Waal equation?

    A. $P(V-nb) = nRT$
    B. $(P + an^2/V^2) = nRT$
    C. $P = an^2RT/(V^2-nb)$
    D. $P = nRT/(V-nb) - an^2/V^2$

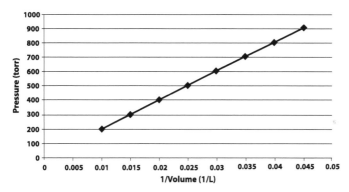

1 atm = 760 torr

R = 0.08206 atm-L/mol-K

22. How many moles of gas are in this sample? (Hint: PV = slope of graph)
    A. 893 mol
    B. 1.17 mol
    C. 2.2 x 10⁻⁶ mol
    D. 13.6 mol

UNIT 7

Questions 23–27

A phase diagram describes the physical state of an element or compound at differing pressures and temperatures. The lines on the diagram represent phase boundaries, and a change in conditions that crosses those boundaries will result in a phase change. The solid state is at the upper left, at high pressure and low temperature. The gas phase is at the bottom, at low pressure. The liquid phase is in the upper right, at high temperature and pressure. At temperature and pressure above the terminus of the liquid-gas phase boundary, the critical point, the substance becomes a supercritical fluid, with the gas and liquid phases indistinguishable from one another.

The diagram below is a generic phase diagram that will be used in each of the following questions.

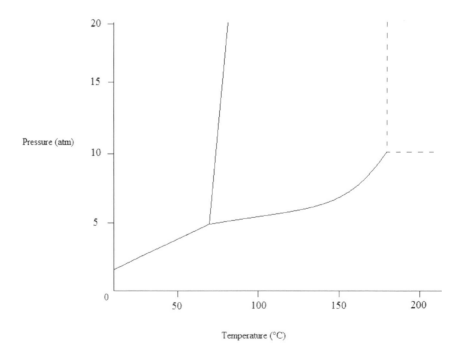

23. At what temperature and pressure conditions do all three phases of the material coexist?

    A. 2 atm, 95°
    B. 5 atm, 120°
    C. 8 atm, 40°
    D. 5 atm, 70°

24. In what form would the compound be at atmospheric pressure and room temperature?

    A. solid
    B. liquid
    C. gas
    D. supercritical fluid

25. At a constant temperature of 50°, decreasing the pressure on the substance from 5 atmospheres to 2 atmospheres would result in what physical process?

    A. sublimation
    B. deposition
    C. evaporation
    D. fusion

26. Based on the diagram, what statement can be made about the relative densities of the solid and liquid phases of this material?

    A. The liquid phase is denser than the solid phase.
    B. The solid phase is denser than the liquid phase.
    C. Both the solid and liquid phases are equally dense.
    D. No statement can be made based on the diagram.

27. Which of the following is closest to the vapor pressure of the material at 150°?

    A. 4 atm
    B. 6 atm
    C. 8 atm
    D. 10 atm

UNIT 8

Questions 28-32

A buffer is a solution of a weak acid and its conjugate base which is very useful for controlling the pH of a system. For example, the pH of blood is held around 7.4 by a buffer system of carbonic acid and its conjugate base, bicarbonate.

A buffer works by reacting with any acidic or basic molecules that enter the system and neutralizing them. Where a strong acid or base greatly changes the pH of a non-buffered solution, the buffer can absorb the new molecules with much less of a change because only the weak acid or base remains active and can affect pH. The buffer capacity is the point at which the added acid or base has reacted with all of the buffer acid (for added bases) or base (for added acid), and the buffer can no longer control the pH.

The pH of a buffer system is governed by the Henderson-Hasselbach equation, which relates the pH to the pK_a of the acid and the log of the ratio between the concentrations of base and acid. The most effective buffers are those with a ratio close to 1:1, giving them the most buffer capacity in either direction.

$$pH = pK_a + \log \left({}^{conc.\ base}\!/_{conc.\ acid} \right)$$

Acid	Conjugate Base	pKa
acetic acid	acetate	4.76
carbonic acid	bicarbonate	6.37
hypochlorous acid	hypochlorite	7.5
ammonium	ammonia	9.25
phenol	phenoxide	9.99

28. Which of the acids in the table would be best suited for preparing a buffer at a pH of 8.0?

    A. carbonic acid
    B. acetic acid
    C. phenol
    D. hypochlorous acid

29. If the blood is buffered at a pH of 7.4, what is the approximate ratio of bicarbonate to carbonic acid in the blood?

    A. 100:1
    B. 10:1
    C. 1:1
    D. 1:10

30. Which of the following is closest to the pH of an ammonium buffer system with an acid:base concentration ratio of 5:1?

    A. 7.5
    B. 8.5
    C. 9.5
    D. 10.5

31. A solution buffered with acetic acid to a pH of 5 would be able to absorb more:

    A. base, because there is more acetate than acetic acid in the buffer.
    B. base, because there is more acetic acid than acetate in the buffer.
    C. acid, because there is more acetate than acetic acid in the buffer.
    D. acid, because there is more acetic acid than acetate in the buffer.

32. If 10 mmol of phenol are dissolved in water, about how much sodium hydroxide must be reacted with it to prepare a buffer at a pH of about 10?

    A. 1 mmol
    B. 9 mmol
    C. 11 mmol
    D. 5 mmol

Organic Chemistry: UNIT 1

Questions 1–3

There are more than fifty kinds of steroid produced by the adrenal glands. Not all of them are secreted into the blood stream. The more important ones are those that exist in the veins of the adrenal glands and possess physiological functions. There are nine different kinds of steroid found in the veins of the adrenal glands. Adrenocortical hormones must contain 18, 19, or 21 carbons and have the following general structure.

For those with only 18 carbons, the ring containing carbons 1-5 must be a benzene ring, and a carbon (carbon 18) must be bonded to carbon 13. For those with 19 carbons, carbons 10 (carbon 19) and 13 (carbon 18) must each have an extra carbon bonded to them. For those with 21 carbons, they must have the same structure as those with 19 carbons, plus a two carbon chain bonded to carbon 17 (carbons 20 and 21). Glucocorticoids, such as cortisone, moderate the metabolism of sugar, fats, and proteins. Cortisone like molecules must have 21 carbons.

These structures must contain an oxygen base at carbon 11. In addition, carbon 20 must have a carbonyl group, and carbon 21 must contain an oxygen base. Cortisone or corticosteroids are widely used in medicine. They control allergies, inflammation, and many disease processes. Cortisone compounds can be applied to the skin in the form of creams, or taken internally. A variety of pharmaceutical derivatives of cortisone have been developed.

1. In order for a pharmaceutical derivative of Cortisone to be effective, it must contain the structural requirements of a glucocorticoid. Which of the following molecules would not be a suitable corticosteroid pharmaceutical?

A.

C.

B.

D.

2. An androgen is a steroid hormone that controls the development and maintenance of masculine secondary sex characteristics. Conversely, estrogen is a steroid hormone that controls the development and maintenance of feminine secondary sex characteristics. The 18 carbon adrenocortical hormones include the estrogens and the 19 carbon hormones contain the androgens. Which of the following molecules could be utilized as the estrogen component of birth control pills?

A.

C.

B.

D.

Anabolic steroids are synthetic substances that mimic the male sex hormones

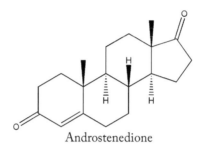

Androstenedione

3. What statement is true about the above molecule?

   A. Androstenedione is not an anabolic steroid because it has a methyl group attached to carbons 10 and 13

   B. Androstenedione is not an anabolic steroid because it has oxygen attached to carbons 3 and 17

   C. Androstenedione is an anabolic steroid because it has oxygen attached to carbons 3 and 17

   D. Androstenedione is an anabolic steroid because it has a methyl group attached to carbons 10 and 13

UNIT 2

Question 4

The cardiac glycosides are an important class of naturally occurring drugs whose actions include both beneficial and toxic effects on the heart. Plants containing cardiac steroids have been used as poisons and heart drugs at least since 1500 B.C. Throughout history these plants or their extracts have been variously used as arrow poisons, emetics, diuretics, and heart tonics. Cardiac steroids are widely used in the modern treatment of congestive heart failure and for treatment of atrial fibrillation and flutter. Yet their toxicity remains a serious problem. The general structure of the cardiac glycosides includes a steroid component and a sugar component. The structure of the steroid portion is similar to the general structure of the adrenocorticoids, except a butaryolactone ring or pyrone ring will be attached to carbon 17. A methyl group must be attached to carbon 13. The glycoside must be attached to an O bonded to carbon 3.

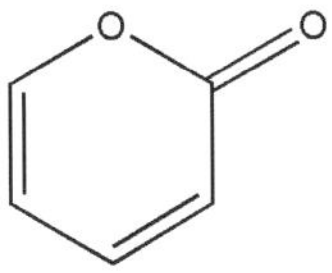

Pyrone ring 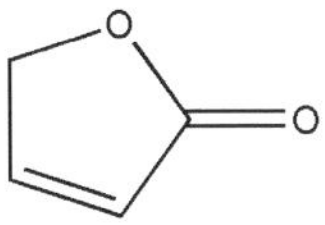   Butaryolactone ring

4. The Christmas Rose is a highly toxic plant used in Africa to poison the tips of arrows. Its toxin is made up of a highly potent cardiac glycoside. Which of the following structures could represent the toxin?

A.

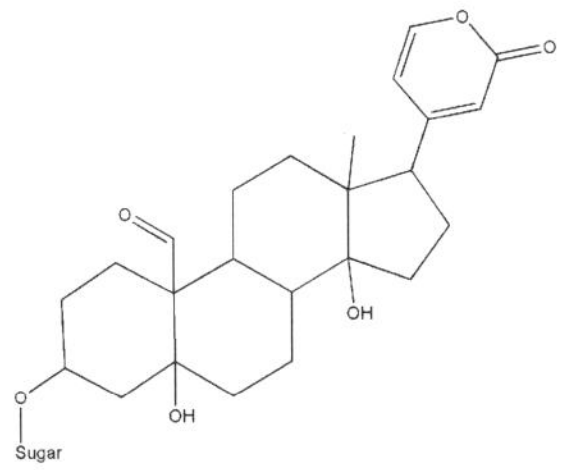

C.

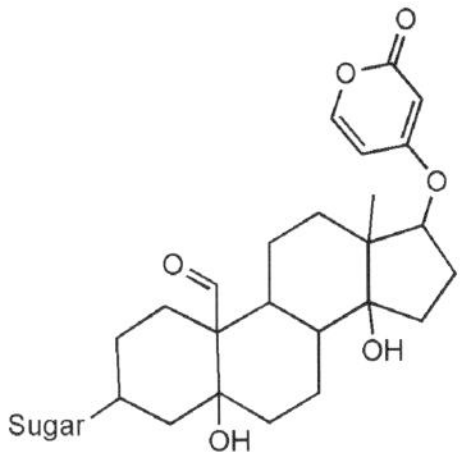

B.

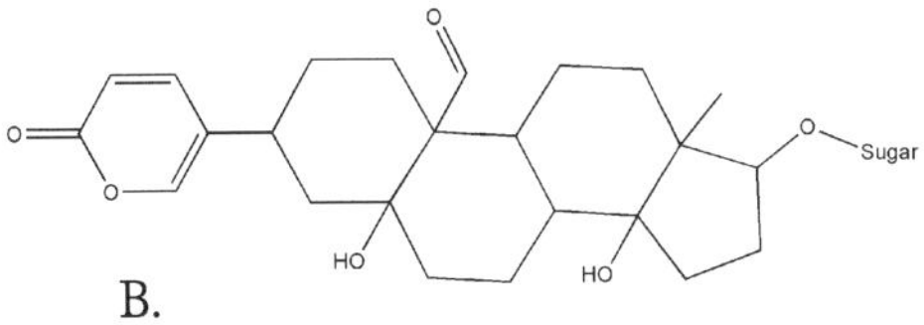

D.

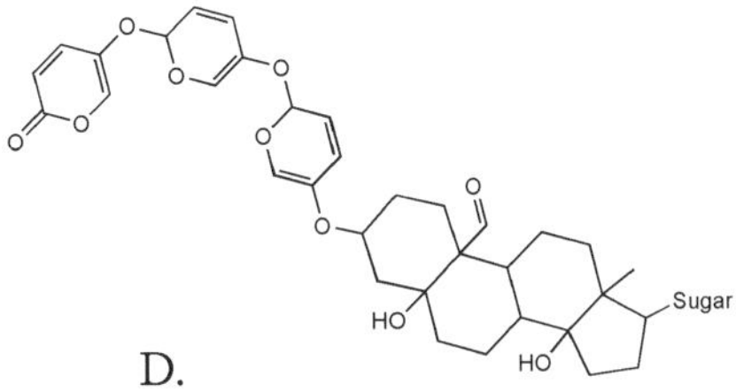

UNIT 3

Questions 5-8

Fatty acids consist of the elements carbon (C), hydrogen (H) and oxygen (O) arranged as a carbon chain skeleton with a carboxyl group (-COOH) at one end. Saturated fatty acids have no double bonds between the carbons, and thus the chain is said to be saturated by the H's attached to the C. Monounsaturated fatty acids have only one double bond, while polyunsaturated fatty acids have more than one double bond.

Below is a table listing a series of common fatty acids and their respective chemical formulas

Acid	Formula
Palmitic	$C_{16}H_{32}O_2$
Palmitoleic	$C_{16}H_{30}CO_2$
Linoleic	$C_{18}H_{32}O_2$
Oleic	$C_{18}H_{34}O_2$
Stearic	$C_{18}H_{36}O_2$
Arachidic	$C_{20}H_{40}O_2$
Gadoleic	$C_{20}H_{38}O_2$
Arachidonic	$C_{20}H_{32}O_2$
Behenic	$C_{22}H_{44}O_2$
Erucic	$C_{22}H_{42}O_2$
Docosahexaenoic	$C_{22}H_{32}O_2$

5. The general chemical formula for the fatty acids is as follows:

$$CH_3(CH_2)_n(CH=CHCH_2)_m(CH_2)_pCOOH$$

What are n, m, and p for Oleic Acid?
   A. 3, 3, 5
   B. 4, 2, 6
   C. 8, 0, 8
   D. 7, 1, 6

Omega-3 and Omega-6 fatty acids are unsaturated essential fatty acids because they must be included in the diet because the human metabolism cannot make them from other fatty acids. Linolenic acid is an Omega-6 fatty acid because it has a double-bond three carbons away from the last carbon in the chain, also known as the omega carbon. The classification of an omega fatty acid can be obtained by subtracting the highest double-bond locant in the scientific name from the number of carbons in the fatty acid. So for linolenic acid, it would be 18-12 = 6. All double bonds in omega fatty acids are in the cis configuration.

linoleic acid

6. Given that arachidonic acid is an omega fatty acid, which of the following represents the structure of arachidonic acid?

A.

C.

B.

D.

7. If n = 7, what type of Omega fatty acid is oleic acid?

   A. Omega-3

   B. Omega-6

   C. Omega-9

   D. Omega-12

8. Increases in intermolecular interactions between the hydrocarbon chains of fatty acids results in an increase in the melting point of the fatty acids. Which is the correct order of increasing melting temperature from lowest to highest of the following fatty acids.

   i.   Docosahexaenoic acid

   ii. Arachidic acid

   iii. Behenic acid

   iv. Arachidonic acid

   A. ii < iv < iii < i

   B. iv < i < ii < iii

   C. i < iv < iii < ii

   D. iii < ii < iv < i

UNIT 4

Questions 9–12

Anandamide is a member of a family of nitrogen containing fatty acid derivatives found in a variety of different organ systems in the body. It is a natural agonist of the cannabinoid receptors, which can be activated by Δ^9-tetrahydrocannabinol or THC, the active ingredient in marijuana. Agonistic and antagonistic binding to the cannabinoid receptors has been associated with a variety of therapeutic applications including treatment of nausea, as an analgesic, reduced anxiety, increased or decreased feeding behaviour, treatment of movement disorders such as Parkinson's disease, treatment of glaucoma, cancer treatments, and treatment of cardiovascular disease, among others. In addition to anandamide, a variety of other fatty acid ethanolamides have been implicated in cannabinoid receptor binding. In the laboratory, these compounds can be synthesized by a simple two-step method which involves the activation of a fatty acid followed by reaction with ethanolamine as shown below:

STEP 1: Activation of fatty acid

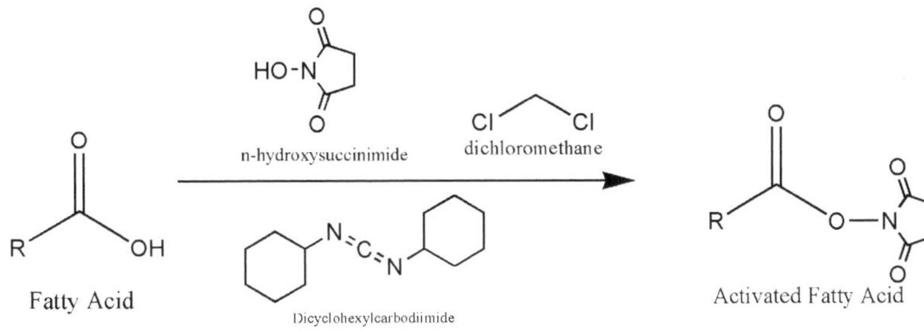

STEP 2: Reaction with ethanolamine

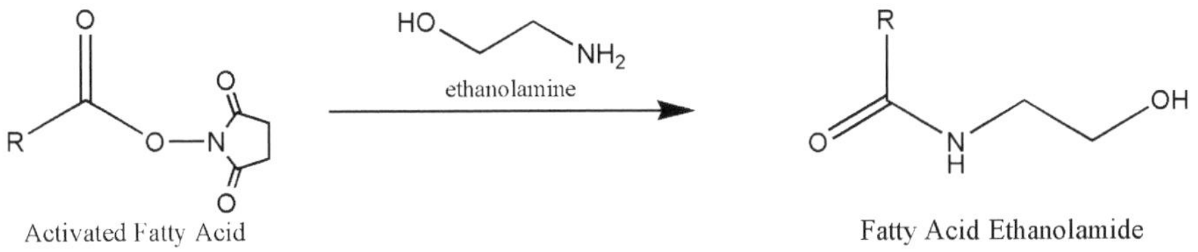

Anandamide can be made from arachidonic acid, which has the following structure

arachidonic acid

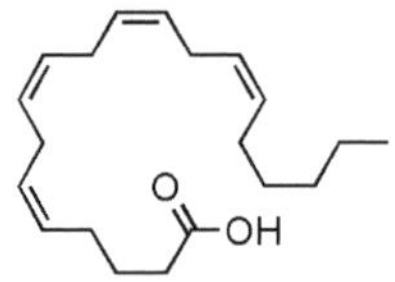

9. Which of the following structures represents anandamide?

A.

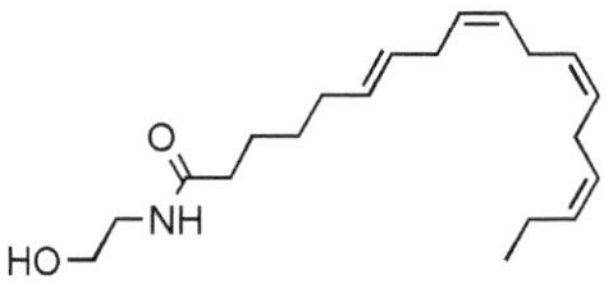

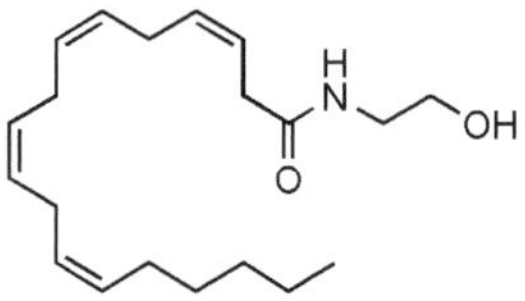

C.

B.

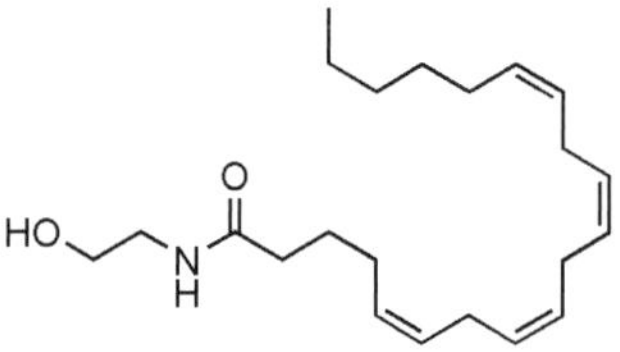

D.

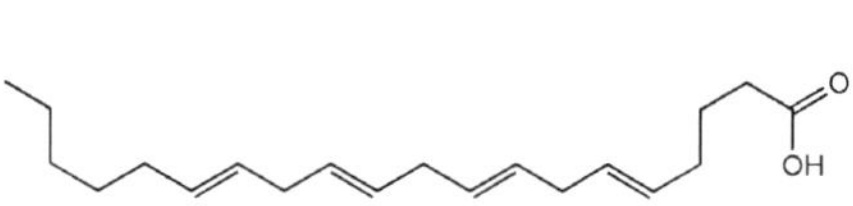

10. In addition to the production of a fatty acid ethanolamide in the above reaction, the dicyclohexylcarbodiimde forms an unwanted side product by reacting with the water released during the activation step. This product forms a white precipitate. Which of the following represents the side product formed?

A.

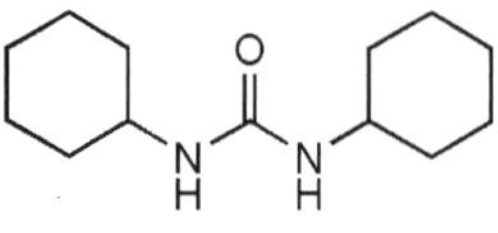

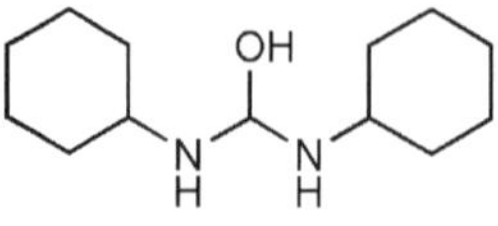

C.

B.

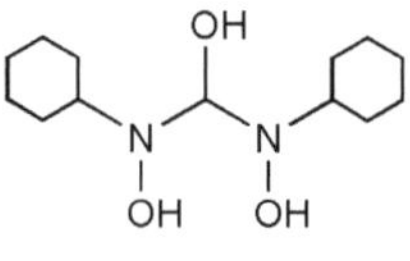

D.

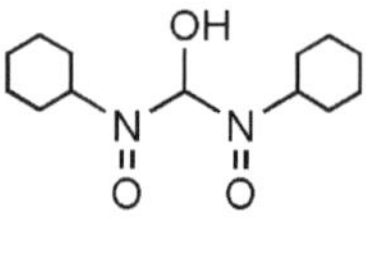

Molecules such as fatty acid ethanolamides that have a hydrophilic portion and hydrophobic portion are known as surfactants.

11. Which of the following molecules could be attached to a fatty acid to produce a surfactant?

I.

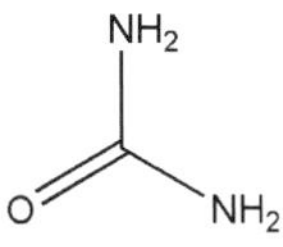

NH$_2$

O   NH$_2$

II.

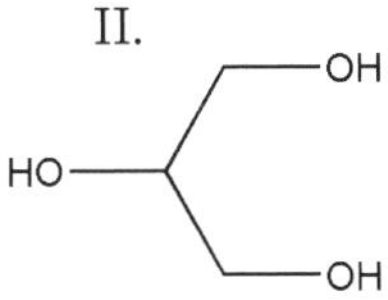

HO

-OH

-OH

III. CH$_3$

Br

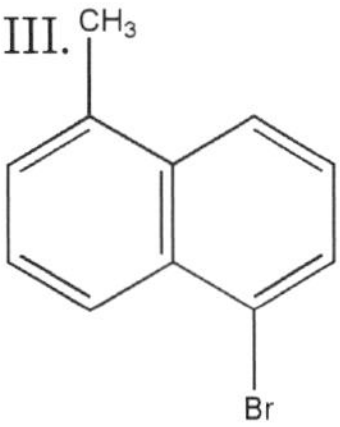

A. I only
B. II and III
C. I and III
D. I and II

12. Oleamide can be synthesized with a similar reaction used to create fatty acid ethanolamides. The structure of oleamide is

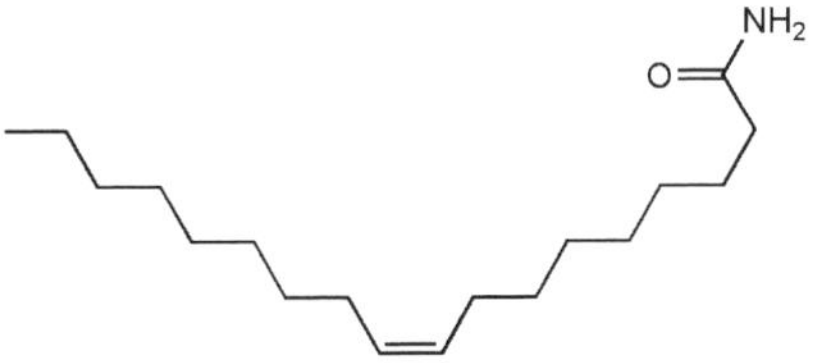

NH$_2$

O

oleamide

What molecule would you need to react activated oleic acid with in the second step to produce the above molecule?

A.   NH$_3$

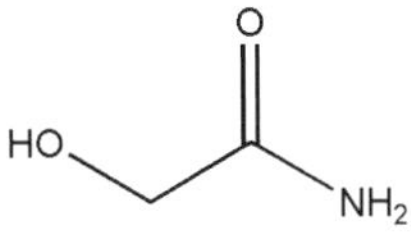

C.   HO   NH$_2$

B.   HO   NH$_2$

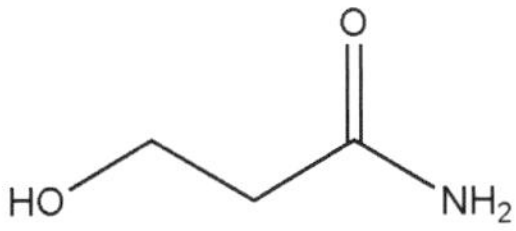

D.   HO   H$_2$N

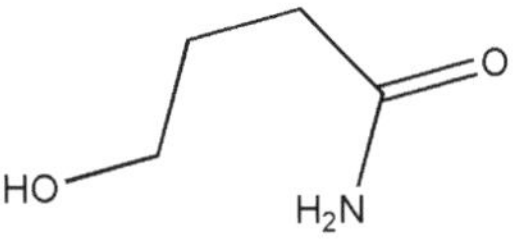

UNIT 5

Questions 13–16

Most syntheses of nitrogen heterocycles involve substitution and/or condensation reactions of nitrogen nucleophiles with halide or carbonyl compounds. In the synthesis of nitrogen heterocycles, regioselectivity is usually not an issue since the nitrogen reagents react symmetrically. In addition, the formation of heteroaromatic systems is thermodynamically favourable, and can therefore be achieved under acidic or oxidative conditions. Oxygen as a substituent on nitrogen heterocycles tends to be double-bonded.

The following reaction resulting in the loss of water from the reactants is an example of the formation of a nitrogen heterocycle.

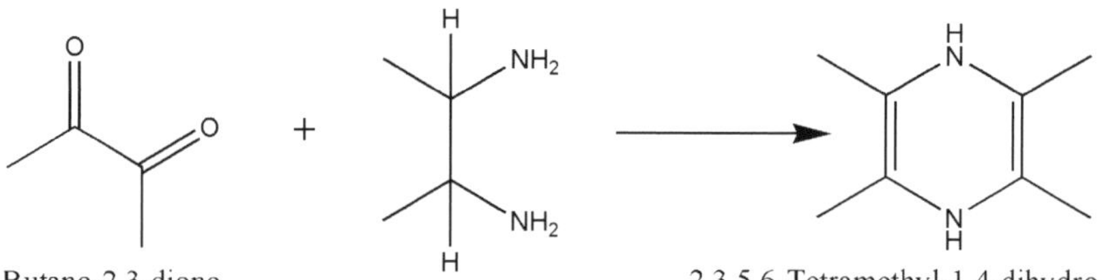

Butane-2,3-dione   +   Butane-2,3-diamine   →   2,3,5,6-Tetramethyl-1,4-dihydro-pyrazine

Upon oxidation, the product becomes

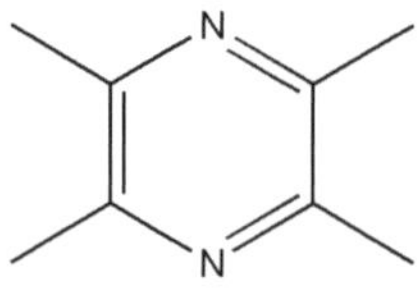

2,3,5,6-Tetramethyl-pyrazine

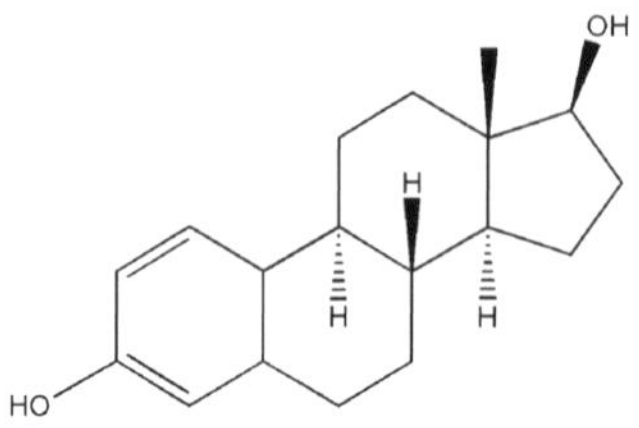

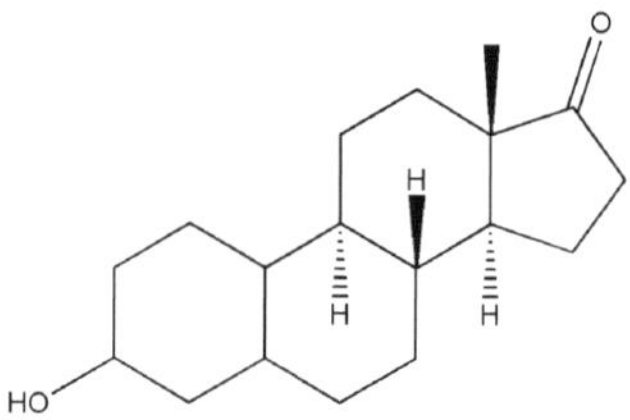

13. Which of the following molecules could you react butane-2,3-diamine with to obtain the same product?

A.

C.

B.

D.

14. If butane-2,3-diamine was reacted with what would be the resulting product?

A.

C.

B.

D.

15. In the above reaction, what molecule is lost during the synthesis of the nitrogen heterocycle?

    A. Cl_2
    B. HCl
    C. NH_3
    D. COOH

16 Which molecule is represented by P in the following equation?

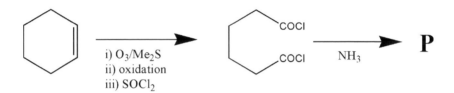

A.

C.

B.

D.

UNIT 6

Questions 17–20

Alkenes are hydrocarbon chains containing one or more C=C double bonds. The smallest of the alkenes, ethene (ethylene), is a plant hormone which controls growth, seed germination, and fruit development. Other alkenes function as pheromones for insect communication including sex, alarm, and trail pheromones. They can be formed by an elimination reaction of an alcohol in a strong acid or an alkyl halide in a strong base.

Alkenes have the general structure

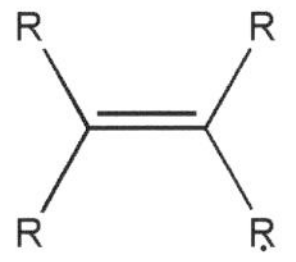

In order to synthesize ethene, ethanol could be reacted with a strong acid, resulting in

$$H_2C \!=\! CH_2$$
ethene

17. Ethene can also be made from bromoethane (CH_2CH_2Br). Which of the following molecules would be necessary to synthesize ethene from bromoethane?

   A. H_2SO_4
   B. H_2O
   C. KOH
   D. Both A and C could be used

18. Given 2-bromodecane, which of the following alkenes would be formed by an elimination reaction?

A.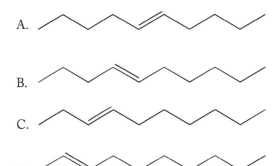

B.

C.

D.

19. An addition reaction is the opposite of an elimination reaction. What would be the result of an addition reaction of the following with HCl?

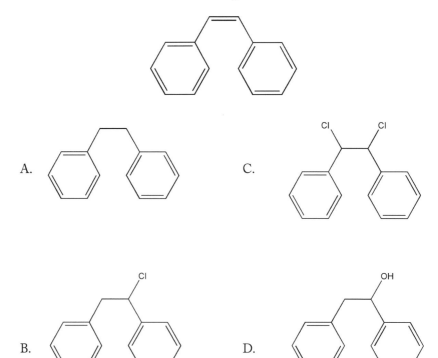

A.

B.

C.

D.

20. If an alkene is unsymmetrical, there is the possibility of two different products from an HX addition (X represents any halide), however one product will predominate. Markovnikov's rule states that in additions of HX to unsymmetrical alkenes, the H^+ of HX goes to the double-bonded carbon that already has the greatest number of hydrogens. Which of the following statements regarding Markovnikov's rule is true?

    A. The H^+ is more likely to bond with the carbon with the most H's because there is less steric hindrance on that carbon

    B. The H^+ is more likely to bond with the carbon with the most H's because it yields the most stable carbo cation intermediate

    C. The H^+ is more likely to bond with the carbon with the most H's because it yields the least stable carbo cation intermediate

    D. The H^+ is more likely to bond with the carbon with the most H's because there is more steric hindrance on that carbon

UNIT 7

Questions 21 - 24

Hemiacetals have the following general structure:

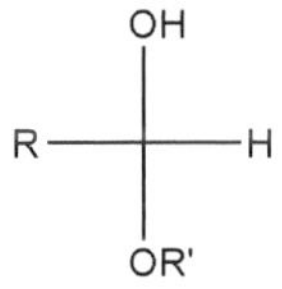

OH
|
R——————H
|
OR'

Hemiacetal

In most cases, hemiacetals are not stable and the aldehyde or ketone form having the following structure is generally favoured.

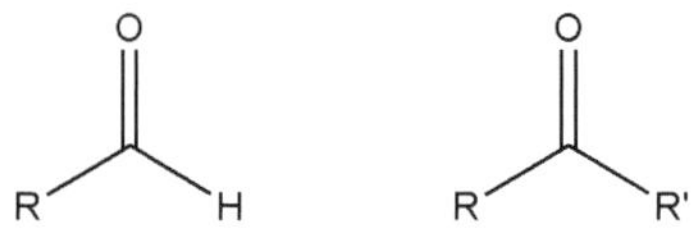

Aldehyde   Ketone

However, when a molecule has on OH group γ or δ to an aldehyde or ketone carbonyl group, the molecule undergoes an intra-molecular reaction to form a five or six-membered hemiacetal ring as shown.

These types of molecules are extremely important since glucose and other sugars contained in this configuration will form cyclic hemiacetal in water.

21. Which of the following molecules contains a hemiacetal group?

I.

II.

III.

A. I
B. II.
C. III.
D. I. and III.

22. Which two structures would be formed when the following molecule forms a hemiacetal ring?

A.

B.

C.

D.

23. What would be the most stable form of the following molecule?

A.

B.

C.

D.

24. A hydrate which can be formed from an aldehyde or a ketone has the following general structure

Hydrate

Given the following three molecules:

I.

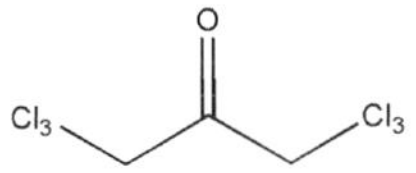

II.

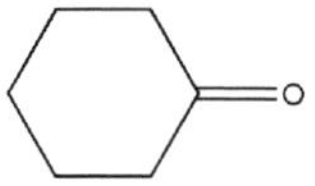

III.

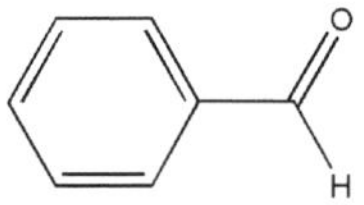

Which of the above structures would form the most stable hydrate?

A. I

B. II

C. III

D. None of them would form hydrates

UNIT 8

Questions 25–27

Imines (compounds that contain C double-bonded to N) are important intermediates in the biological synthesis of amino acids, which are used in the synthesis of proteins. In cases where an organism's diet does not contain the necessary amounts of required amino acids, the organism can in some cases convert an unneeded amino acid to a desired one using the transamination reaction. This process involves the transfer of an amino group from the unneeded amino acid to a keto group as shown:

| old amino acid | old keto acid | new amino acid | new keto acid |

This process occurs through a series of imine intermediates

25. Which structure represents the new amino acid formed by the following transamination?

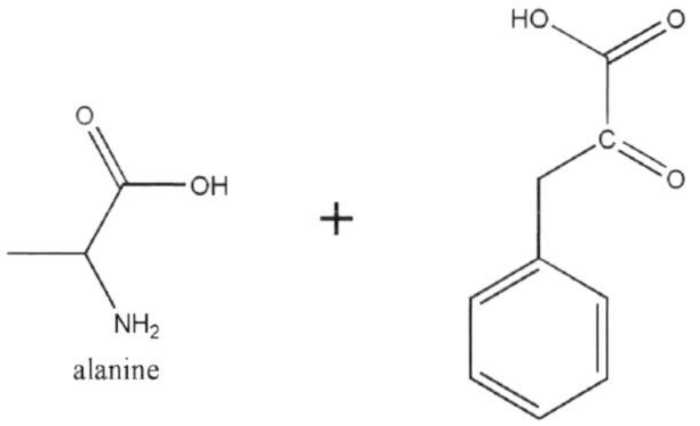

alanine

+

2-Oxo-3-phenyl-propionic acid

A.

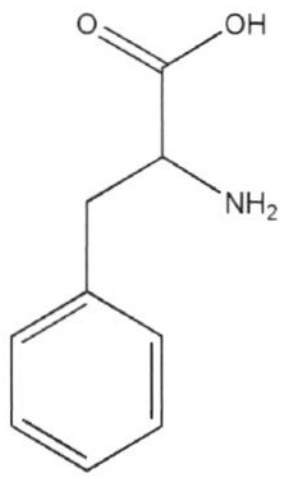

C.

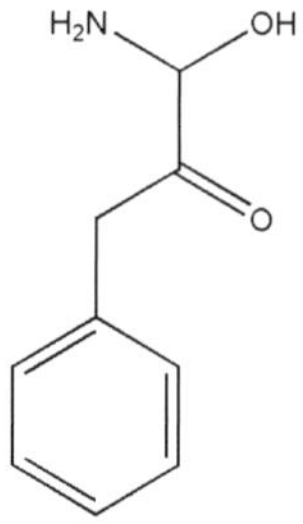

B.

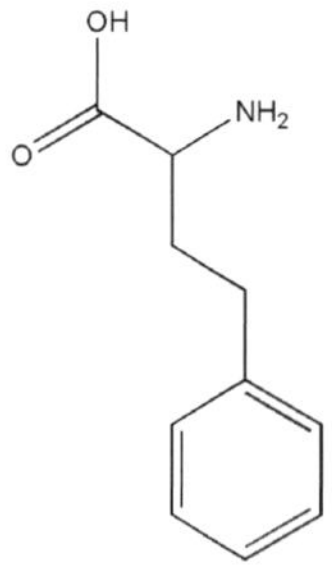

D.

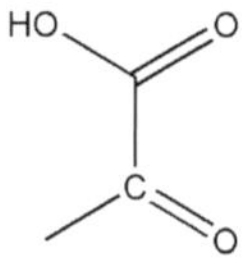

26. Which of the following molecules are possible intermediates in the transamination process?

I.

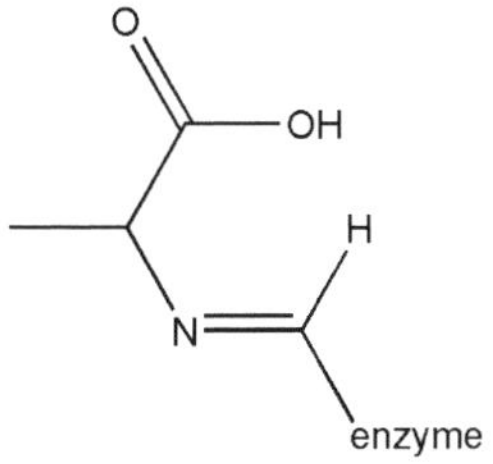

II.

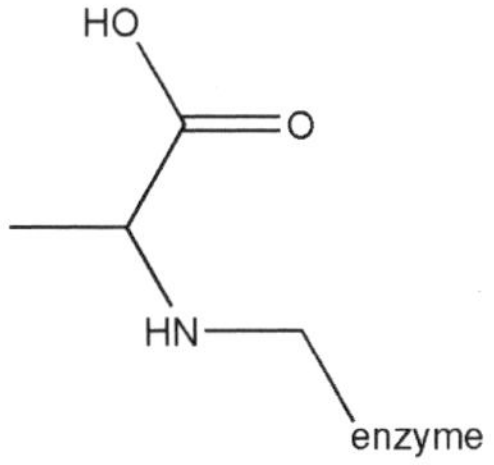

III.

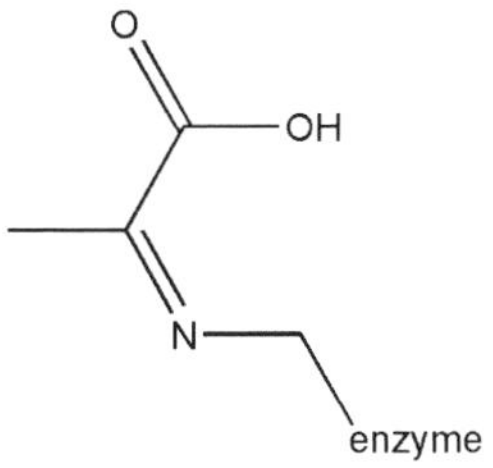

IV.

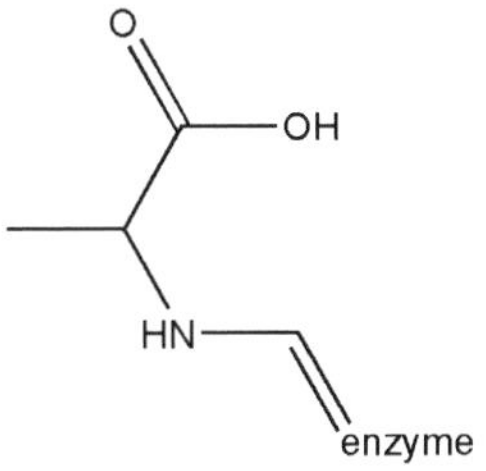

A. I and II

B. I, II, IV

C. II and IV

D. I and III

27. Threonine is one of the 9 essential amino acids that humans must have in their diet. Given a supply of serine, what molecule would be necessary to form this essential amino acid through transamination?

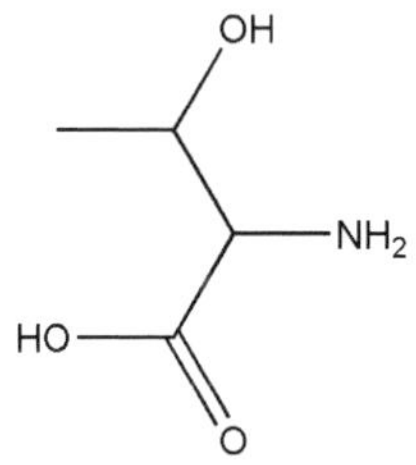

threonine

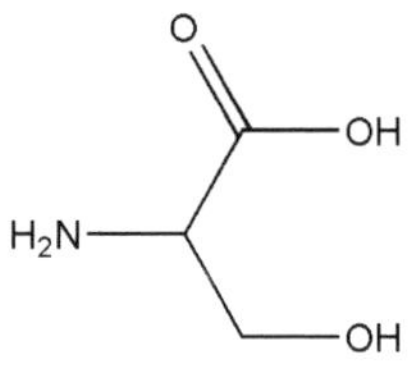

Serine

A.

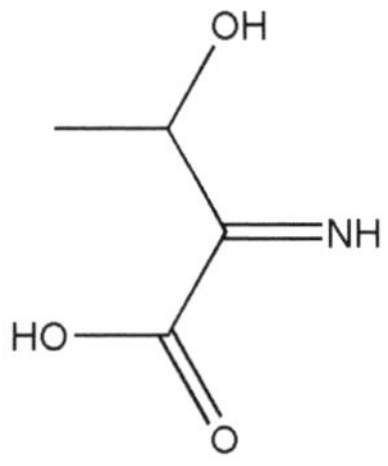

C.

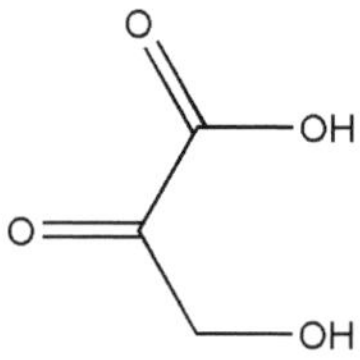

B.

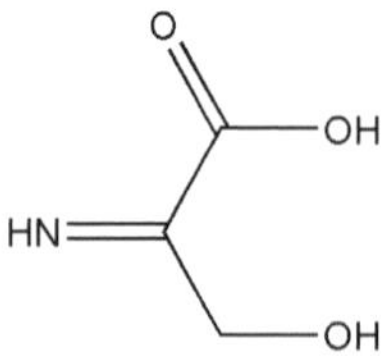

D.

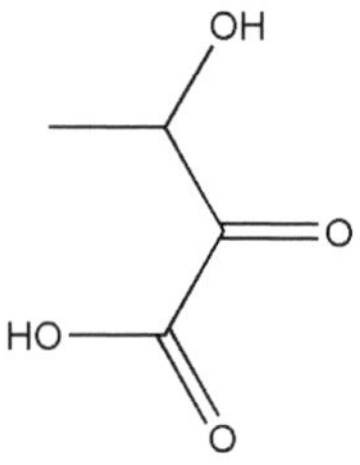

UNIT 9

Questions 28 - 31

A carbonyl compound with acidic alpha hydrogen may exist in two forms called tautomers, a special type of inter-convertible structural isomers that differ from each other only in the location of a double bond and a hydrogen atom relative to oxygen.

O
R'
R
OH
R'
R

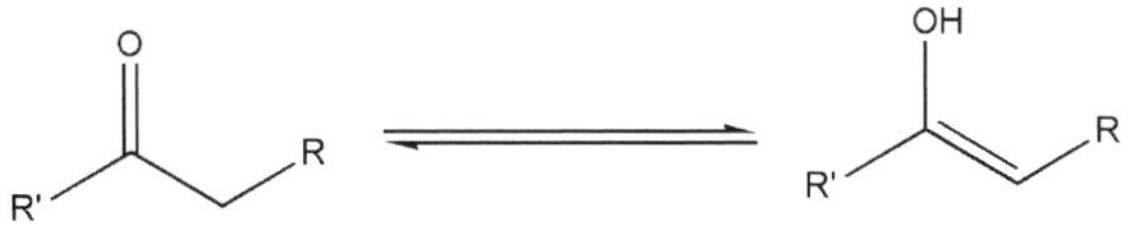

Keto form Enol form

Tautomers are extremely important in the formation of the DNA double helix because it is necessary for the bases to take the keto form in order for hydrogen bonding to occur.

28. Which set of base pairs demonstrates correct hydrogen bonding (represented by dashed lines) between the two molecules?

A.

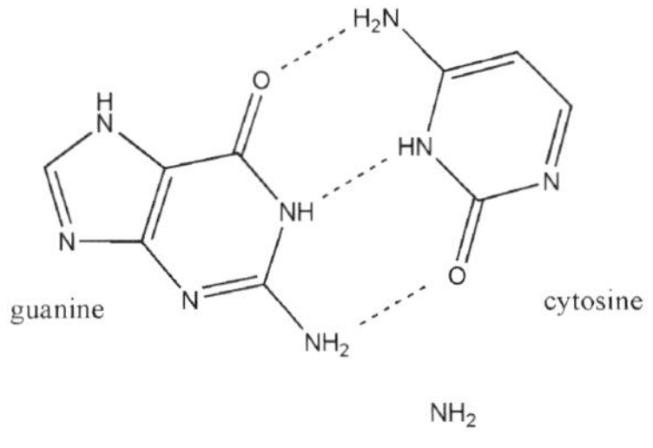

H
N
N
O
NH
N
NH2
H2N
HN
N
O
guanine
cytosine
NH2

C.

H
N
N
OH
NH
N
NH2
H2N
HN
N
O
guanine
cytosine

B.

H
N
N
OH
N
N
NH2
H2N
N
N
HO
guanine
cytosine

D.

H
N
N
O
NH
N
NH2
H2N
N
N
HO
guanine
cytosine

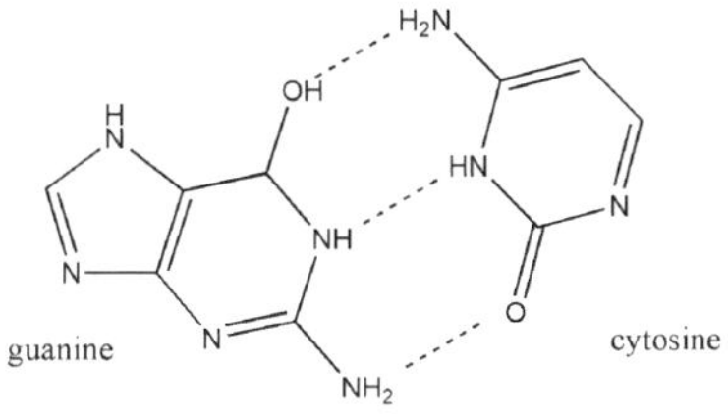

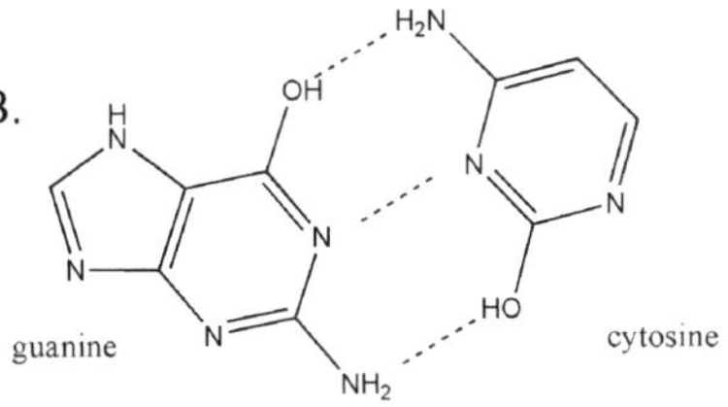

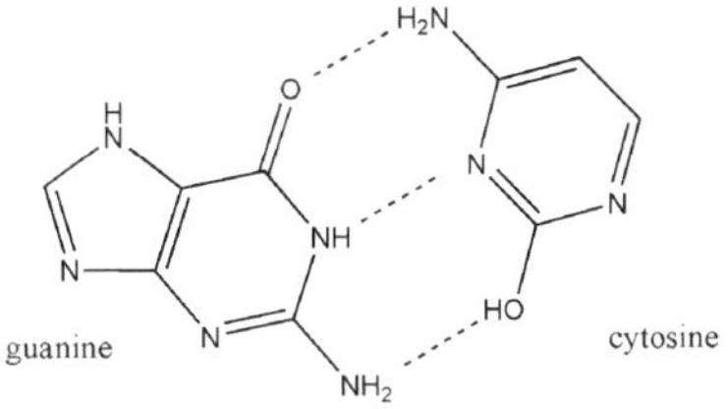

29. In the metabolism of carbohydrates, the first step is the breakdown of glucose in the digestive tract. In this first step, glucose 6-phosphate is formed followed by isomerism to fructose 6-phosphate. This isomerism is simply a tautomerization that proceeds through a specific intermediate.

glucose 6-phosphate   fructose 6-phosphate

Which of the following represents the intermediate form for this tautomerization?

A.

B.

C.

D.

30. The hydrogen alpha to a carbonyl group is acidic. This is primarily because of resonance stabilization of the enolate ion. An enolate is an anion derived by loss of hydrogen from the alpha carbon of a carbonyl group; it is the anion of an enol. Which of the following hydrogens are acidic?

    I. $CH_3CH=CHCHO$

    II. C_6H_5CHO

    III. $CH_3CH_2CO_2CH_2CH_3$

A. I and II
B. II
C. III
D. II and III

31. Given the following equilibrium mixture of enolates, which would be present in the greatest amount?

    A.   B.

A. Compound A
B. Compound B
C. Both compounds would be present in equal amount
D. Neither compound is an enolate and therefore the above equilibrium would not exist

UNIT 10

Questions 32 - 36

The Cahn Ingold Prelog priority rules are used to determine the orientation of a molecule for purposes of assigning stereochemistry at the stereocenter, a carbon with 4 different attached groups. Simply put, any atom attached to a stereocenter has a Cahn Ingold Prelog priority corresponding to its atomic number – the higher the atomic number, the higher the priority. After the substituents of a stereocenter have been assigned their priorities, the molecule is so oriented in space that the group with the lowest priority is pointed away from the observer. If the lowest priority substituent is assigned the number 4, and the highest 1, then the sense of rotation of a route passing through 1, 2 and 3 distinguishes the stereoisomers. A center with a clockwise sense of rotation is an R or *rectus* center and a center with an anticlockwise sense of rotation is an S or *sinister* center, two molecules with the same chemical structure, but different directions of rotation are known as diastereomers. Notice how when the NH_2 changes from out of the plane of the paper to into the plane of the paper, the rotation changes in the molecule.

R   S

Ephedrine and pseudoephedrine, both of which are used as decongestants, are diastereomers.

ephedrine   pseudoephedrine

The only difference between these two molecules is the OH group, which the solid wedge indicates it is coming out of the plane of the paper for ephedrine, while the dashed wedge indicates it is going into the plane of the paper for the pseudoephedrine. These molecules have two stereo centers. By using the rules of priority, the O would get the highest priority (4), the phenyl ring would get next highest (3), the other C would be next (2), and finally the H would get lowest priority. In the case of the second stereo center, the N would have highest priority (4), and again the H the lowest, while the C-O would be 3, and the methyl would be 2. So for ephedrine, the rotation would be as follows

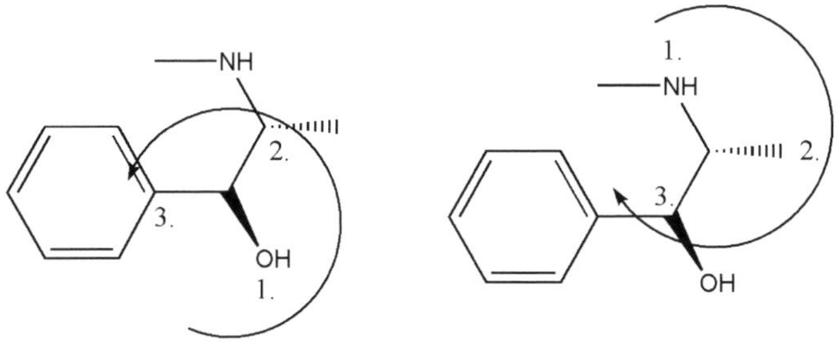

So, ephedrine would have a 1S, 2R arrangement. In contrast, the pseudoephedrine would have a 1R, 2R arrangement (the change at the first stereocenter is due to the OH going into the plane of the paper, so the rotation flips directions).

32. Given the following molecule, how many stereocenters exist?

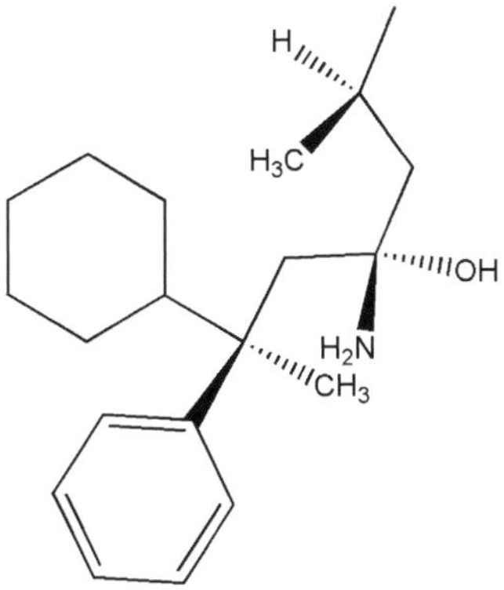

A. 0
B. 1
C. 2
D. 3

33. Which of the following molecules are diastereomers?

A.

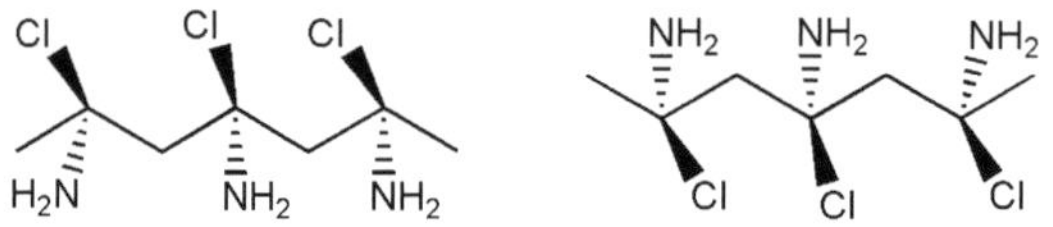

B.

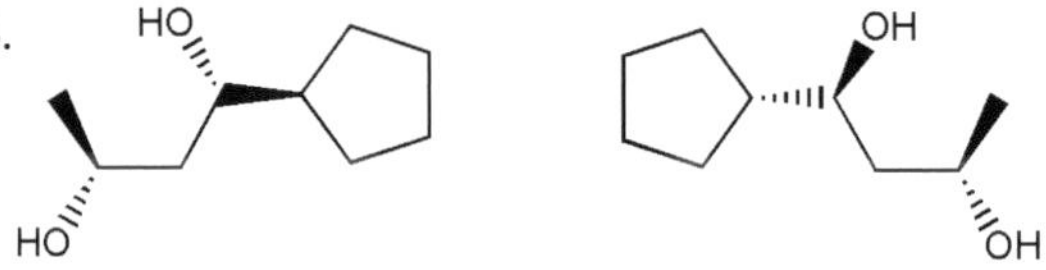

C.

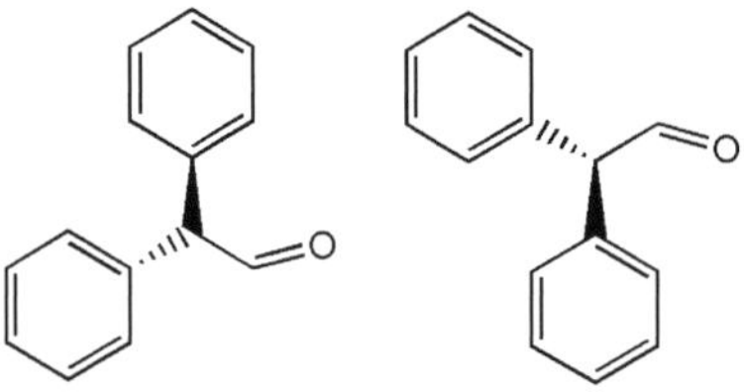

D.

34. How many diastereomers are there of threonine?

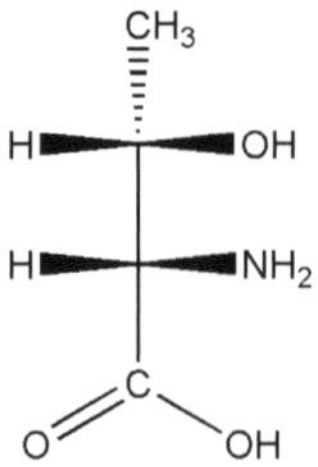

Threonine

A. 1

B. 2

C. 3

D. 4

35. What is the R, S orientation of the following molecule?

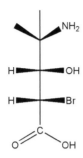

A. 2R,3R
B. 2R,3R,4R
C. 2R,3S
D. 2R,3S,4R

36. Which of the following molecules has a 2S, 3R, 4R configuration?

A.

C.

B.

D.

UNIT 11

Questions 37–41

In organic chemistry, saturation is an important measure of the amount of hydrogen that can be bound by an organic molecule. A saturated molecule is one that has carbons bound to the maximum amount of hydrogen possible, while an unsaturated molecule has one or more points at which it can accept hydrogen atoms. Unsaturation can be counted in a molecule using the formula

$$\frac{2C + N + 2 - H - X}{2}$$

where C is the number of carbon atoms, N is nitrogen, H is hydrogen, and X is any halogen. Oxygen does not count, but any hydrogen bound to it, such as in an alcohol, does count in the formula. Practically, each degree of saturation from the formula represents a single element within the structure, either a ring or a π-bond. That is, each ring and double bond is one degree of unsaturation, and each triple bond is two degrees of unsaturation.

37. How many degrees of unsaturation are in the molecule shown?

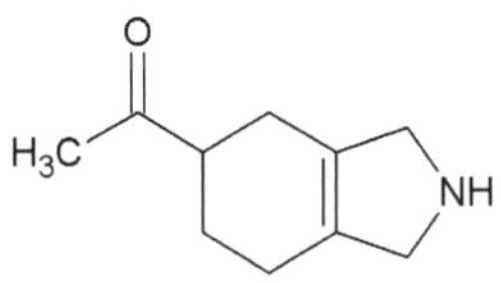

   A. 2
   B. 3
   C. 4
   D. 5

38. Which of the following structures contains exactly 3 degrees of unsaturation?

A

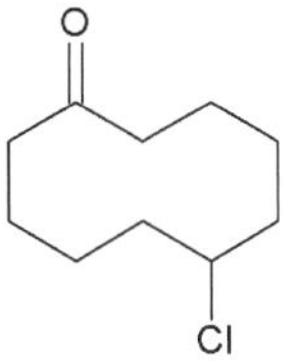

B

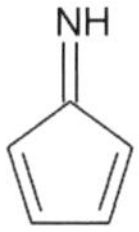

NH

C

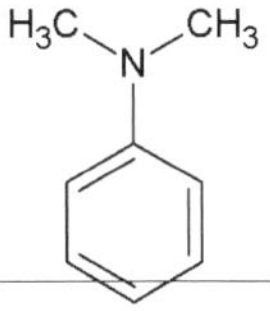

H₃C   CH₃
    N

D

H₃C
    CH₃

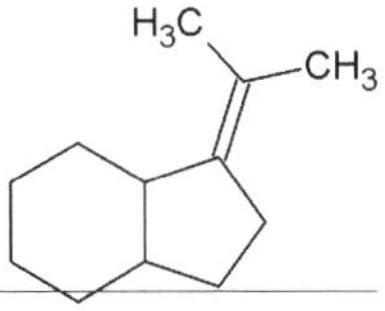

39. How many degrees of unsaturation are present in a molecule with the formula $C_7H_5N_3O_6$?

A. 5
B. 6
C. 7
D. 8

40. Which of the following molecular formulas contains exactly 2 degrees of unsaturation?

A. $C_5H_{14}N_2O$
B. $C_7H_{13}NO_2$
C. $C_6H_{12}O_6$
D. $C_6H_{12}N_2C_{12}$

41. How many different saturated molecular structures can be formed with the formula C_6H_{14}?

A. 4
B. 5
C. 6
D. 7

UNIT 12

Questions 42–46

One of the most common methods of representing the electronic structure and bonding patterns of molecular species is Lewis structures. In Lewis structures, the atoms in a molecule or multiatomic ion are first laid out in the shape of the molecule, then the valence electrons and ion charge, if present, are distributed in pairs throughout the molecule to satisfy the octet rule (in most cases) and minimize formal charge. Formal charge is calculated by subtracting the number of unshared electrons and half the number of bonding electrons for each atom from its number of valence electrons. If formal charge is necessary, electronegativity and resonance stabilization generally determines where it is placed.

Spatial structure can also be determined from the Lewis structure using the valence shell electron-pair repulsion model (VSEPR), which maximizes the angle between the as shown in the table. The bond angles are determined by the total number of lone pairs and σ-bonds on the atom.

Electronic Structure	Geometry	Bond Angle
2 Bonds	linear	180°
3 Bonds	trigonal planar	120°
2 Bonds, 1 Lone Pair	bent	120°
4 Bonds	tetrahedral	109°
3 Bonds, 1 Lone Pair	trigonal pyramidal	109°
2 Bonds, 2 Lone Pairs	bent	109°
5 Bonds	trigonal bipyramidal	120°,90°
4 Bonds, 1 Lone Pair	see-saw	120°,90°
3 Bonds, 2 Lone Pairs	T-shape	90°
6 Bonds	octahedral	90°
5 Bonds, 1 Lone Pair	square pyramidal	90°
4 Bonds, 2 Lone Pairs	square planar	90°

42. Which structure for the cyanate ion is the most stable?

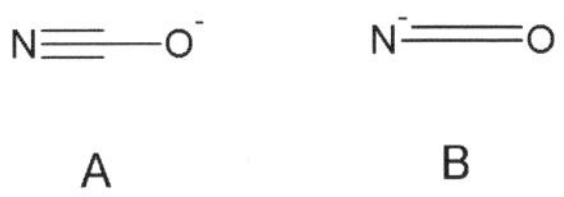

$$N \equiv\!\!-O^{-} \qquad N^{-}\!\!=\!\!=O$$

    A   B

A. A, because oxygen is more electronegative than nitrogen
B. A, because nitrogen is more electronegative than oxygen
C. B, because oxygen is more electronegative than nitrogen
D. B, because nitrogen is more electronegative than oxygen

43. Which of the following molecules cannot be drawn without formal charge?

A. H_2SO_4
B. CH_3Br
C. O_2
D. O_3

44. What is the hydrogen-oxygen-hydrogen bond angle in water?

A. 90°
B. 109°
C. 120°
D. 180°

45. What is the molecular geometry of the chlorine center of the perchlorate ion, ClO_4^-?

A. tetrahedral
B. square planar
C. see-saw
D. square pyramidal

46. Which of the following species does not obey the octet rule?
A. $COCl_2$
B. NO^-
C. BF_3
D. CO_2

Physics: UNIT 1

Questions 1 – 5

Radioactive decay is a process by which a nucleus, generally one of a heavy, unstable element, undergoes a transformation and in doing so emits a radioactive particle. The three primary forms of nuclear decay are α, β, and γ. In alpha decay, a heavy nucleus transforms into a lighter nucleus by emitting a radioactive α particle consisting of two protons and two neutrons. In beta decay, a nucleus changes into an element with either one more or one less proton by converting a neutron into a proton or vice versa. To conserve charge, a tiny β particle with negligible mass and a charge opposite that of the change is emitted; in β- decay, where the atomic number increases by 1, the β particle is an electron. In gamma decay, the only change within the nucleus is a proton's transition to a lower energy state, so the radiated γ particle is a photon, a massless packet of electromagnetic energy.

1. The β- particle is an electron; what is the β+ particle, which has the same mass but a charge of +1?

    A. a positron
    B. a proton
    C. a neutron
    D. a neutrino

2. An α particle is identical to what atomic nucleus?

    A. hydrogen
    B. deuterium
    C. tritium
    D. helium

3. $^{242}_{94}Pu$ α decays to what element?

    A. $^{240}_{92}U$
    B. $^{238}_{92}U$
    C. $^{240}_{90}Th$
    D. $^{238}_{90}Th$

4. Which form of electromagnetic radiation is closest in energy to gamma radiation?

    A. radio waves
    B. microwaves
    C. x-rays
    D. visible light

5. A $^{252}_{99}$Es nucleus undergoes β+ decay. What is the mass number of the resulting nucleus?

    A. 250
    B. 251
    C. 252
    D. 253

UNIT 2

Questions 6-10

Stars are primarily classified based on their temperature, along with several other factors such as color and luminosity. All of these are related to the specific chemistry of the nuclear fusion reaction that is taking place at the core of each star. The Hertzsprung-Russell diagram shows a series of stars, arranged by surface temperature and relative luminosity, with the Sun shown for reference. Most stars spend the majority of their life cycle in the main sequence fusing hydrogen and converting their fuel into massive amounts of energy. The luminosity on the scale is relative to that of the Sun; luminosity is measured in terms of absolute magnitude (M), the intrinsic brightness of a star which can be related to apparent magnitude (m), its visible brightness, by the equation $M = m - 5 \times [(\log D) - 1]$, where D is the distance in parsecs to the star.

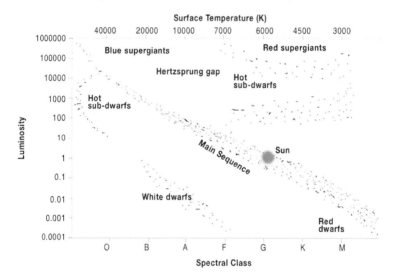

6. According to the diagram, what color star would have a surface temperature of 15000 K and a relative luminosity of 0.01?

    A. yellow
    B. white
    C. red
    D. blue

7. Which of the following types of star is the densest?

   A. neutron star
   B. red giant
   C. white dwarf
   D. protostar

8. A certain star, initially massing 2×10^{30} kg, fuses hydrogen at a rate of 6 trillion kg per second. About how long will it take the star to burn through all of its hydrogen fuel?

   A. 300 million years
   B. 1 billion years
   C. 10 billion years
   D. 25 billion years

9. What is the product of the hydrogen fusion reaction which powers stars in the main sequence?

   A. iron
   B. oxygen
   C. carbon
   D. helium

10. The supergiant star Canopus, the second-brightest star in the nighttime sky, is located 96 parsecs from the Earth and has an apparent magnitude of -0.72. Which of the following is closest to its absolute magnitude?

   A. -1.5
   B. -3.5
   C. -5.5
   D. -7.5

UNIT 3

Questions 11–15

In a direct-current or DC circuit, electrical energy flows in the form of current though a closed loop. The current is driven by a source of electric potential difference, or voltage drop, and is inversely proportional to the resistance of the circuit as governed by Ohm's Law, $V = I \times R$. The total resistance of a circuit depends on the configuration of resistors. Resistors in series combine additively, where $R = R_1 + R_2 + R_3...$; resistors in parallel combine in a reciprocal fashion, where $1/R = 1/R_1 + 1/R_2 + 1/R_3$, etc. Voltage and current, on the other hand, determine the electrical power of a DC circuit according to the equation $P = I \times V$.

11. What is the total resistance of a DC circuit that includes a 3 Ω resistor in series with a pair of parallel 3 Ω resistors?

   A. 4.5 Ω
   B. 6.0 Ω
   C. 7.5 Ω
   D. 9.0 Ω

12. What is the voltage drop across an 8 Ω resistor with a 2 A current flowing through it?

   A. 4 V
   B. 6 V
   C. 10 V
   D. 16 V

13. What current is produced by a 10 V battery connected to a pair of 1 Ω resistors in series?

   A. 2 A
   B. 5 A
   C. 10 A
   D. 20 A

14. How much electrical energy is carried in one second by a 20 A current flowing through a 5 Ω resistor?

    A. 80 J
    B. 400 J
    C. 2000 J
    D. 4000 J

15. A DC circuit is composed of three identical resistors, all connected in parallel; a 12 V battery placed in series with the resistor group is producing 6 A of current in the circuit. What is the resistance of each resistor?

    A. 2 Ω
    B. 4 Ω
    C. 6 Ω
    D. 8 Ω

UNIT 4

Questions 16–20

Lenses work by taking advantage of the law of refraction, which states that any light ray passing between two substances changes direction at an angle dictated by the difference in their indices of refraction. The index of refraction n measures the speed of light in any material as compared to its speed in a vacuum, according to the equation $n = {}^c/_v$, where c is the speed of light in vacuum and v is its speed in the material. Lenses bend light in such a way that an object viewed through a lens will appear to be in a different location, at the image. The image distance i and object distance o are related by a constant called the lens focal length f, where $1/f = 1/o + 1/i$. For converging lenses, the image is on the opposite side of the lens from the object and is a real image; for diverging lenses the image is on the same side as the object and is a virtual image. The magnification of an image can be calculated as $M = {}^{-i}/_o = {}^f/_{f-o}$. A positive magnification means that the image is upright compared to the object, while negative magnification means that it is inverted.

16. If an object is at a distance of 100 cm from a lens with a focal length of 50 cm, at what distance from the lens will the image appear?

    A. 25 cm
    B. 50 cm
    C. 100 cm
    D. 200 cm

17. If a convex lens with a focal length of 30 mm forms an image 45 mm from the lens, what will be the magnification of the image produced?

    A. -1.5
    B. -0.5
    C. 0.5
    D. 1.5

18. In the previous question, what type of image is formed?

    A. virtual and upright
    B. virtual and inverted
    C. real and upright
    D. real and inverted

19. What is the approximate speed of light in water (n = 1.33)?

    A. 200,000 $km/_s$
    B. 225,000 $km/_s$
    C. 300,000 $km/_s$
    D. 400,000 $km/_s$

20. The approximate speed of light in glass is 200,000 $km/_s$. What is the refractive index of glass?

    A. 1.25
    B. 1.33
    C. 1.5
    D. 1.67

SOLUTIONS- BIOLOGY

UNIT 1

Questions 1–3

Question 1

STEP 1 => What do you need to determine to solve the problem?
You need to determine the heart rate from the given ECG. You are given an ECG, and a description of the different waves in the ECG

STEP 2 = > What relevant data provided in this problem is necessary in order to answer the question?
From the passage, you know that each large square horizontally represents 200 ms. You also know that a complete heart beat encompasses a PQRST wave complex, so that the distance from the peak of one wave to that same wave in the next beat would represent exactly 1 heart beat.

STEP 3 = > Use the relevant data to solve the question
Since you know that each large square is 200 ms, all you need to do is count the number of squares from the peak of a wave in one beat, to the peak of that same wave in the next beat and then calculate the time for each beat. Since the R wave is the largest peak, it is the easiest to follow. When the number of big squares between successive R waves is counted, it is found that there are approximately 5 between successive waves. This means that the heart beats once every second. Multiply by 60, and you get 60 beats per minute, or answer B.

Question 2

STEP 1 => What do you need to determine to solve the problem?You need to determine the systolic beat from the given ECG.

STEP 2 = > What relevant data provided in this problem is necessary in order to answer the question?
From the passage, you are told that the P wave represents atrial contraction, and the QRS wave represents ventricular contraction. The systolic beat is simply the part of the heart beat which occurs when the heart is contracting. You know that each large square represents 200 ms.

STEP 3 = > Use the relevant data to solve the question
Now, simply examine how many large squares it takes to complete a PQRS wave. A PQRS wave encompasses slightly less than 2 large squares, so the time is just less than 400 ms. Note, the answers are in seconds, so it is necessary to convert. Therefore, the correct answer is A, 0.35 s = 350 ms.

Question 3

STEP 1 = > What do you need to determine to solve the problem?
You need to determine the peak voltage at the skin from the given ECG

STEP 2 = > What relevant data provided in this problem is necessary in order to answer the question?
From the passage, you know that each large square vertically represents 10 mV. You are also given an explanation as to how an ECG works to measure the charge separation between at least 2 electrodes to give a voltage. The ECG reading is just a graphical representation of these voltage changes over time.

STEP 3 = > Use the relevant data to solve the question
You are looking for peak voltage, so examine the largest peak on the given ECG (an R wave). You can see that the R waves extend through 2 full large squares and a little more than half of another large square. Again, be careful with your units as the answer is given in volts and you are measuring in mV. So since a large square equals 10 mV, the peak occurs at just slightly greater than 25 mV. So, examining the answers, C is the correct answer since 0.026 V = 26 mV.

UNIT 2

Questions 4–7

Question 4

STEP 1 = > What do you need to determine to solve the problem?
When does the bat consume a blood meal

STEP 2 = > What relevant data provided in this problem is necessary in order to answer the question?
You are given a graph which shows the change in bat's urine osmo-concentration and bat's urine production over time. The passage states that before consumption of a meal, the bat is in a drought state, but after consumption, the system adjusts to a flood condition by producing a large amount of dilute urine.

STEP 3 = > Use the relevant data to solve the question
From the passage, you know that as soon as the blood meal is consumed, urine production will increase dramatically. Therefore, by examining the graph, you can see that the peak in urine production occurs after about 20 mins on the graph, so the answer is B.

Question 5

STEP 1 = > What do you need to determine to solve the problem?
How does the bat counter the increase in body weight that results from consuming a blood meal

STEP 2 = > What relevant data provided in this problem is necessary in order to answer the question?
Again, examine the given graph which shows the change in bat's urine osmo-concentration and bat's urine production over time. The passage states that before consumption of a meal, the bat is in a drought state, but after consumption, the system adjusts to a flood condition by producing a large amount of dilute urine.

STEP 3 = > Use the relevant data to solve the question
Since you know that the bat adjusts to the flood condition brought on by the consumption of blood, you know that the increase in weight brought on by the large amount of blood consumed can be countered by excreting a large volume of urine. By examining the graph, you can see that the urine volume increases to a maximum about 20 minutes after the point when the feeding begins, so the answer is A.

Question 6

STEP 1 = > What do you need to determine to solve the problem?
How does the vampire bat offset the large evaporative water loss that occurs due to flying

STEP 2 = > What relevant data provided in this problem is necessary in order to answer the question?
Again, examine the given graph which shows the change in bat urine osmoconcentration and bat urine production over time. In addition, the passage states that over the next hour or so, urine volume decreases while concentration increases to up to 20 times that of plasma.

STEP 3 = > Use the relevant data to solve the question
The graph shows that the increase in urine concentration corresponds to a rapid decrease in urine production, such that when concentration is highest, urine production is lowest. Therefore, by increasing the urine concentration, the bat can effectively conserve water so the answer is D.

Question 7

STEP 1 = > What do you need to determine to solve the problem?
Why is it necessary for the bat to convert its waste product to urea instead of ammonia.

STEP 2 = > What relevant data provided in this problem is necessary in order to answer the question?
You are told in the passage that the bat converts its waste to urea, and in the question that waste products produced from amino acids are ammonia, urea, and uric acid.

STEP 3 = > Use the relevant data to solve the question
This question requires a bit of reasoning, rather than gaining information from the passage. So use the process of elimination. Answer A is incorrect because the stability of the molecule would have no effect on the bat's ability to excrete it. Answer C is incorrect because the urine removed after feeding is quite diluted, so the urea concentration would be very low. From the passage, you know that the bat increases its urine concentration to conserve water and from the graph you know that when urine concentration increases, urine production decreases. Thus it wouldn't make any sense that urea would assist in urine production. Answer D is also incorrect. Ammonia is a small molecule NH_2, thus it wouldn't make any sense that it would require excess energy to excrete it. Therefore, the answer is B. This answer is very reasonable since the passage states that concentration increases up to 20 times that of plasma. At such a high concentration, the waste product would have to be non-toxic.

UNIT 3

Questions 8-10

Question 8

STEP 1 = > What do you need to determine to solve the problem?
Why are gamma rays used in nuclear imaging

STEP 2 = > What relevant data provided in this problem is necessary in order to answer the question?
The passage states that, the most common forms of radiation include gamma rays, alpha rays, beta rays, X rays, and positrons. In addition, a description of the different forms of radiation is provided. In relation to gamma rays, the passage says that: gamma rays (g) does not consist of particles, it is similar to X-rays but of higher energy. During gamma decay, the nucleus falls down to a lower energy state and a photon (sometimes called a gamma particle) is released.

STEP 3 = > Use the relevant data to solve the question
With the exception of the X-rays and the gamma rays, the rest of the forms of radiation are simply particles. A wave would be much more penetrating than a particle. In addition, the passage states that gamma rays have higher energy than X-rays. So the answer is C, since the higher energy and the fact that it is a wave rather than a particle will affect its penetrating ability.

Question 9

STEP 1 = > What do you need to determine to solve the problem?
The type of radioactive decay occurring in the given radioactive reaction.

STEP 2 = > What relevant data provided in this problem is necessary in order to answer the question?
$H^3 \rightarrow He^3$ + radioactive particle. You are told that when alpha decay occurs, high speed helium nuclei is produced. With Beta decay, a neutron is turned into a proton and an electron (beta particle) is released. With positron emission, a proton is turned into a positron and a neutron and the positron is emitted. And with gamma decay, During gamma decay, the nucleus falls down to a lower energy state and a photon is released.

STEP 3 = > Use the relevant data to solve the question
So, examine the reaction and determine what is occurring. In this case, the H^3 would need to gain a proton to become He^3. Therefore, the H^3 has undergone beta decay, answer D.

Question 10

STEP 1 = > What do you need to determine to solve the problem?
What would the result of the alpha decay of plutonium-239 be?

STEP 2 = > What relevant data provided in this problem is necessary in order to answer the question?
The passage tells you that during alpha decay a high speed He nuclei is produced. This means that a He-4 is released

STEP 3 = > Use the relevant data to solve the question
So, subtracting 4 from the AW of plutonium-239, you get 235. Since there is a decrease in AW of Pu, the atom changes to U. So, the answer is A.

UNIT 4

Questions 11-14

Question 11

STEP 1 = > What do you need to determine to solve the problem?
How much of an element with a half-life of 2 days is left after 6 days

STEP 2 = > What relevant data provided in this problem is necessary in order to answer the question?
You are told in the passage that the half-life is the time it takes for a given radioactive isotope to lose half of its radioactivity

STEP 3 = > Use the relevant data to solve the question
This question is pretty straight forward; the amount of an element that has a half-life of 2 days will be cut in half 3 times over 6 days. Thus, the amount left will be equal to ½ x ½ x ½ = 1/8. The answer is C.

Question 12

STEP 1 = > What do you need to determine to solve the problem?
You need to determine the biological half-life of ^{99m}Tc

STEP 2 = > What relevant data provided in this problem is necessary in order to answer the question?
You are told in the passage that the rate of decrease of radiation exposure is affected by both the physical and biological half-life, giving an effective half-life for the isotope in the body. Though the biological half-life cannot be expected to be as precise as the physical half-life, it is useful to compute an effective half-life from

$$1/T_{Effective} = 1/T_{Physical} + 1/T_{Biological}$$

In addition, the question provides you with the effective and physical half-life of ^{99m}Tc

STEP 3 = > Use the relevant data to solve the question
Use the formula and watch your units

From the question
Physical half-life = 6 hrs = 0.25 days
Effective half-life = 0.2 days

So $1/0.2 = 1/0.25 + 1/T_{Biological}$
$5 = 4 + 1/T_{Biological}$
$T_{Biological}$ = 1 day = answer C

Question 13

STEP 1 = > What do you need to determine to solve the problem?
How much ^{32}P will remain after 53 days 3 hrs?

STEP 2 = > What relevant data provided in this problem is necessary in order to answer the question?
Again, you will need the formula
$1/T_{Effective} = 1/T_{Physical} + 1/T_{Biological}$

In addition, you are told that
Biological half-life = 257 days
Physical half-life = 14 days

STEP 3 = > Use the relevant data to solve the question
So, first you must calculate the effective half-life
$1/T = 1/257 + 1/14$
$T_{Effective}$ = 13.28 days
Now, convert 53 days 3 hrs to days = 53.13 days

Find out how many half-lives have occurred in this time
13.28/53.13 = 4
So, the amount left = $0.5 \times 0.5 \times 0.5 \times 0.5$ = 1/16 = answer D

Question 14

<u>STEP 1 = > What do you need to determine to solve the problem?</u>
Which statement is true?

<u>STEP 2 = > What relevant data provided in this problem is necessary in order to answer the question?</u>
See solution 20
In addition, you are told that ^{90}Sr has a long half-life and that it mimics calcium in the body

<u>STEP 3 = > Use the relevant data to solve the question</u>
From the passage, you can interpret that it is necessary for the body to rid itself of a radioactive element either via excretion, or the short physical half-life of the element. With ^{90}Sr, you are told that it has a long physical half-life. In addition, because it mimics calcium, it is apparent that it will bind to bone in the body making it difficult to excrete. Thus, the correct answer is B. It will have long biological half-life and when combined with the long physical half-life, it can remain in the body for a long time (in the case of ^{90}Sr, it is 30 years!).

UNIT 5

Questions 15-17

Question 15

STEP 1 = > What do you need to determine to solve the problem?
50 offspring produced, how many will have benign tumors

STEP 2 = > What relevant data provided in this problem is necessary in order to answer the question?
You are told in the passage that malignant tumor is recessive. You are told a benign tumor will be developed when the fish is heterozygous. Using the Punnett square method, you have two parents, one with homozygous dominant, and one with heterozygous genes. Thus, you have parents with TT and Tt, where T is the dominant trait for no tumor, and t is the recessive trait for a malignant tumor.

STEP 3 = > Use the relevant data to solve the question
Make a Punnett square

TT x Tt	T	T
T	TT	TT
t	Tt	Tt

So, the offspring will be 50% homozygous dominant and 50% heterozygous. Therefore, from 50 offspring, approximately half will develop benign tumors, answer B.

Question 16

STEP 1 = > What do you need to determine to solve the problem?
Two parents with benign tumors, 20 offspring, what is the outcome

STEP 2 = > What relevant data provided in this problem is necessary in order to answer the question?
See above solution

STEP 3 = > Use the relevant data to solve the question
Make a Punnett square

Tt x Tt	T	t
T	TT	Tt
t	Tt	tt

So, you will get 25% dominant, 50% heterozygous, and 25% recessive
From 20 offspring, that means 5 with no tumors, 5 with malignant tumors, and 10 with benign tumors – answer D.

Question 17

STEP 1 = > <u>What do you need to determine to solve the problem?</u>
Striped fan-tail mated with a black normal tail, possible phenotype

STEP 2 = > <u>What relevant data provided in this problem is necessary in order to answer the question?</u>
A fan-tail is considered a recessive trait, heterozygous results in a normal tail. In the case of color, black and silver are the basic colors, where black is considered recessive. In the case of a heterozygous for black and silver, a silver fish with black stripes is produced

STEP 3 = > <u>Use the relevant data to solve the question</u>
In this case, you have to include both traits in your Punnett square. Also, since one of the parents has a normal tail, you must consider that this trait could be homozygous dominant or heterozygous

So, you will need 2 Punnett squares

Ccff x ccFF	Cf	cf
cF	CcFf	ccFf

50% striped with a normal tail and 50% black with a normal tail

Ccff x ccFf	Cf	cf
cF	CcFf	ccFf
cf	CcFf	ccff

50% striped with a normal tail
25% black with a normal tail
25% black with a fan-tail

The only possible answer from the above Punnett squares is C.

UNIT 6

Question 18-21

Question 18

STEP 1 = > What do you need to determine to solve the problem?
The key here is the words "Structural element"
In addition, it refers to both the passage and the diagram

STEP 2 = > What relevant data provided in this problem is necessary in order to answer the question?
The passage provides extensive information regarding the immune response in the intestine. The best thing to do is to examine what is said about each of the possible answers so that the information doesn't become too overwhelming

Peyer's Patches - contain five or more lymphoid follicles and are found predominantly in the terminal ileum. The centre of the follicle consists of B lymphocytes surrounded by mantles of mixed cellularity. The inter-follicular region contains T lymphocytes.
Intra-epithelial lymphocyte - IELs have been shown to exhibit cytolytic and possibly immuno-regulatory functions through the secretion of a variety of cytokines, suggesting an important role in local immuno-surveillance of the IEC and the regional microenvironment.
Microvilli – increases surface area
M Cells - M cells (MC) in the epithelium transport foreign macromolecules and micro-organisms to antigen-presenting cells within and under the epithelial barrier.

STEP 3 = > Use the relevant data to solve the question
Now, by examining the above, we are looking for STRUCTURE, not function. The microvilli are the only component listed that alter the actual structure of the intestine by increasing surface area. All the other choices involve cells that have some functions, so the answer is C.

Question 19

STEP 1 = > What do you need to determine to solve the problem?
The key is to determine the function of antigen receptor

STEP 2 = > What relevant data provided in this problem is necessary in order to answer the question?
The passage states that the M cells (MC) in the epithelium transport foreign macromolecules and micro-organisms to antigen-presenting cells within and under the epithelial barrier. It then goes on to describe how once the antigen is transported

across, it can come into contact with a number of different immune cells, such as T cells, macrophages, IELs etc... In addition, the diagram shows how an Ag is being transported through the M cells with IELs awaiting and interacting with a foreign molecule.

STEP 3 = > Use the relevant data to solve the question
The correct answer is A. The passage never even discusses about the killing of the invader. In addition, it is not discussing about digestion. This particular passage is discussing about the immune function of the intestine, not digestion, so B and C are incorrect. D is incorrect because the passage clearly states M cells allow ready attachment of luminal particulate antigens (Ag)s to their surfaces, and the diagram clearly shows that the M cells are the ones that phagocytos the Ag.

Question 20

STEP 1 = > What do you need to determine to solve the problem?
The keys words here are DC and persistent infections

STEP 2 = > What relevant data provided in this problem is necessary in order to answer the question?
The passage on DC explains that the DC first captures the antigen, and then receives certain activating signals. They then can present the antigen and interact with the T cells to elicit T cell activation.

STEP 3 = > Use the relevant data to solve the question
According to the passage, in order for DC to function and produce an immune response, they must first uptake the antigen, then activate and mature before they can interact with the T cells. The body would not be able to rid itself of an infection that somehow would block this activation and maturation process. Thus, the correct answer is C.

Question 21

STEP 1 = > What do you need to determine to solve the problem?
The key words are M cells, unique, and intestinal epithelial cells

STEP 2 = > What relevant data provided in this problem is necessary in order to answer the question?
The passage states that unlike the normal gut epithelial cells, M cells allow ready attachment of luminal particulate antigens (Ag)s to their surfaces.

STEP 3 = > Use the relevant data to solve the question
Since the passage states that the M cells allow attachment of antigens and this is unlike normal gut epithelial cells, the correct answer is C.

UNIT 7

Questions 22-27

Question 22

STEP 1 = > What do you need to determine to solve the problem?
Key words are molecule and thrombus blocking the coronary artery

STEP 2 = > What relevant data provided in this problem is necessary in order to answer the question?
The key to all of the questions associated with this passage is interpretation of the diagram. At first glance, it may seem confusing, but a closer look shows a systematic diagram in which certain molecules are necessary for progression to the next step. By simply following the arrows associated with the section of the diagram in question, it should be quite simple to answer the questions

STEP 3 = > Use the relevant data to solve the question
In this question, it is necessary to determine the best method of eliminating the thrombosis from the coronary artery. You are given 4 molecules; simply examine the diagram to discern the function of each of these molecules in the cascade.

Plasminogen – this gets converted to plasmin. Plasmin can then break down a fibrin clot; however, excess plasminogen would be useless unless it was accompanied by an increase in its conversion to plasmin

Heparin – binds to antithrombin which in turn inhibits factors IIa, IXa, Xa, and XIa. This molecule would be useful in inhibiting the cascade and preventing further thrombosis formation, but would do nothing for an already formed thrombus

Factor XIII – this factor aids in stabilization of the fibrin monomer, so administration of Factor XIII would only assist thrombus formation

Tissue plasminogen activator – this molecule converts plasminogen to plasmin. Plasmin is necessary to break up a clot, so the correct answer is D.

Question 23

STEP 1 = > What do you need to determine to solve the problem?
The Key words are deficiency in factor VIII and section of the coagulation cascade

STEP 2 = > What relevant data provided in this problem is necessary in order to answer the question?
Simply locate factor VIII on the diagram

STEP 3 = > Use the relevant data to solve the question
The coagulation cascade is divided into four different sections. Locating factor VIII on the diagram, it is apparent that it is part of the intrinsic pathway, answer B.

Question 24

STEP 1 = > What do you need to determine to solve the problem?
Key words are test and hemophilia A

STEP 2 = > What relevant data provided in this problem is necessary in order to answer the question?
The passage above the question describes 3 different tests and how they all function.

STEP 3 = > Use the relevant data to solve the question
From the previous question, you know that Hemophilia A is caused by a factor VIII deficiency. The PTT examines how long it takes the blood to clot following the blockage of any calcium dependant factors. A deficiency in factor VIII would result in an even longer PTT because it would not function properly in addition to the calcium dependant factors. So test I would be useful. PT involves the addition of tissue factor (TF). TF directly acts factor III, initiating the extrinsic pathway. Since the extrinsic pathway does not involve factor VIII, PT would not be altered for a person with hemophilia A. Finally, TCT, monitors blood clotting following the addition of thrombin. In this case, the test bypasses both the extrinsic and intrinsic pathway and examines the function of the common pathway. Since thrombin is responsible for the conversion of fibrinogen to fibrin, this part of the cascade would not be influenced in any way by factor VIII. Therefore, the answer is A.

Question 25

STEP 1 = > What do you need to determine to solve the problem?
Key words are deficiency, protein C, and protein S

STEP 2 = > What relevant data provided in this problem is necessary in order to answer the question?
Examining the diagram, you see that activated protein C in conjunction with protein S inactive factors Va and VIIIa

STEP 3 = > Use the relevant data to solve the question
Factors Va and VIIIa are necessary for the conversion of X to Xa and the initiation of the common pathway. If these factors were not inactivated, the common pathway would remain activated and thrombus formation would continue. Therefore, the answer is C.

Question 26

STEP 1 = > What do you need to determine to solve the problem?
Key words are factor XIII deficiency and effect on blood clotting

STEP 2 = > What relevant data provided in this problem is necessary in order to answer the question?
Examining the diagram, you see that factor XIII is fibrin-stabilizing factor, and thus is involved in the stabilization of the polymerized fibrin clot which results from the coagulation cascade.

STEP 3 = > Use the relevant data to solve the question
Inadequate fibrin clot stabilization, would cause a clot that easily breaks down, so although the rest of the pathways would be intact, and the blood would clot properly. Once the fibrin clot formed, it would be insufficient and breakdown easily. Thus, the answer is C

Question 27

STEP 1 = > What do you need to determine to solve the problem?
Key words are factor XIII deficiency and coagulation test

STEP 2 = > What relevant data provided in this problem is necessary in order to answer the question?
Once again, you can return to the passage that discussed the three coagulation tests

STEP 3 = > Use the relevant data to solve the question
See solution for question 24, the correct answer is D since all of the coagulation pathways would be intact, and the deficiency would result in unstable fibrin clots.

UNIT 8

Questions 28-29

Question 28

STEP 1= > What do you need to determine to solve the problem?
Key words are surface area and volume

STEP 2 = > What relevant data provided in this problem is necessary in order to answer the question?
This question does not really require any information from the passage, it is simple mathematics

STEP 3 = > Use the relevant data to solve the question
You must be able to come up with two details, the units of area and the units of volume. From basic mathematics, we know that volume equals length X width X height or $V = l$ X w X h, so the units of volume must be some length measurement cubed, so in this case m^3. Similarly, area is equal to length X width or $A = l$ X w. Surface area is simply the sum of the area of all faces of a particular object so it will have the same units as area. In this case it would be m^2. So, the ratio of surface area/volume = m^2/m^3. This means the units would be m^{-1} or answer B.

Question 29

STEP 1= > What do you need to determine to solve the problem?
Wants you to draw on information given in the passage, you must read the answers first to determine what information you are trying to interpret.

STEP 2 = > What relevant data provided in this problem is necessary in order to answer the question?
This question is asking for details about smaller bodies. The paragraph gives you the equation that correlates BMR with LBM. It also says that the BMR of children is high compared to adults

STEP 3 = > Use the relevant data to solve the question
Children have a higher BMR than adults, they will lose energy more quickly and become cold more easily, thus hypothermia is a greater risk for children. According to the Katch-McArdle formula, an increase in LBM produces an increase in BMR, but it is not an exact relationship(i.e. doubling the LBM does not double the BMR). Therefore, smaller bodies consume energy at a relatively higher rate than larger bodies as compared to their mass. The answer is C.

UNIT 9

Questions 30–33

Question 30

STEP 1= > What do you need to determine to solve the problem?
The key words here are mitosis, chromosomes, and visible

STEP 2 = > What relevant data provided in this problem is necessary in order to answer the question?
Examine the diagram given regarding mitosis. This diagram shows a schematic representation of the different phases of mitosis as well as gives a description of them
In addition, the passage states that the stages of mitosis include prophase, prometaphase, metaphase, anaphase, and telophase

STEP 3 = > Use the relevant data to solve the question
You need to determine from the diagram when chromosomes are present. You can discount answer A immediately as the passage clearly states the phases of mitosis and does not include interphase. The correct answer is B, when examining the diagram corresponding to prophase, the chromosomes are clearly noted in the diagram, and since this is the first phase of mitosis, this would be the correct answer.

Question 31

STEP 1= > What do you need to determine to solve the problem?
The key words are cancer and uncontrolled cell growth, and same tissue

STEP 2 = > What relevant data provided in this problem is necessary in order to answer the question?
The question provides 3 samples and tells how many cells in those samples are undergoing mitosis. From the passage, you know that mitosis is nuclear division plus cytokinesis, and produces two identical daughter cells, meaning simply that mitosis is cell division resulting in new cells.

STEP 3 = > Use the relevant data to solve the question
The key to this question is to understand the idea of uncontrolled cell growth. In the case of the three samples described, sample #2 has significantly more cells undergoing division than the other two samples. Given from the question that these three samples are from the same tissue, they should all have similar rates of mitosis. However, a cancerous tissue would have a much greater rate of mitosis than a normal sample of the same tissue. Thus, the answer is B.

Question 32

STEP 1= > What do you need to determine to solve the problem?
Key words are mitosis, meiosis, and incorrect

STEP 2 = > What relevant data provided in this problem is necessary in order to answer the question?
You have two diagrams, one displaying mitosis and one displaying meiosis. In addition, you are told that mitosis is nuclear division plus cytokinesis, and produces two identical daughter cells; while meiosis is a two part (meiosis I and meiosis II) cell division process in organisms that sexually reproduce. Through a sequence of steps, the replicated genetic material in a parent cell is distributed to four daughter cells.

STEP 3 = > Use the relevant data to solve the question
So, once again, examine the answers first, and then refer to the diagrams. The correct answer is B, while the chromosomes line up singly in metaphase II of meiosis and metaphase I of mitosis, during metaphase I of meiosis, the chromosomes line up in pairs. This can be observed in the diagrams

Question 33

STEP 1= > What do you need to determine to solve the problem?
Key words, prophase, mitosis, meiosis, and common

STEP 2 = > What relevant data provided in this problem is necessary in order to answer the question?
Again, simply examine the diagrams and the prophase stage of the two processes closely

STEP 3 = > Use the relevant data to solve the question
The correct answer is C, chromosome condensation. In both diagrams, it show that the chromosomes shorten and thicken during prophase.

UNIT 10

Questions 34–38

Question 34

STEP 1= > What do you need to determine to solve the problem?
The key words are domains, least involvement, and cell adhesion

STEP 2 = > What relevant data provided in this problem is necessary in order to answer the question?
You are told that FN is an ECM protein that can be involved in cell adhesion. In addition, you are provided with a graph of cell adhesion to different fragments of FN

STEP 3 = > Use the relevant data to solve the question
The graph shows cell adhesion for the different fragments, by simply examining this graph. It is immediately apparent that Type I and Type II domains have no significant effect on cell adhesion so the answer is A.

Question 35

STEP 1= > What do you need to determine to solve the problem?
The key words here are domains, contribute most and cell adhesion

STEP 2 = > What relevant data provided in this problem is necessary in order to answer the question?
Again, you must examine the graph, this time a little more closely

STEP 3 = > Use the relevant data to solve the question
Here, you must draw some conclusions from the results; it is obvious from the graph that type III (6-15) and type III (8-15) have the greatest amount of cell adhesion (displaying similar numbers of adherent cells). This indicates that type III (6-7) is of little importance to cell adhesion. Next, examining the domains that have the next greatest amount of cell adhesion, the graph shows that type III (8-12) and type III (5-11) are next. Again, you can gather that the important parts of these molecules are most likely somewhere in the range from 8-11 or possible 12. Now, when 8 and 9 are removed, as illustrated in type III (10-12) cell adhesion drops significantly, and when 10 is removed as in type III (11-15), it drops even further. Thus, the correct answer is B.

Question 36

STEP 1= > What do you need to determine to solve the problem?
The key words are receptor, synergistic effect and multiple domains

STEP 2 = > What relevant data provided in this problem is necessary in order to answer the question?
You are provided with another graph showing different receptors and how they interact with certain type III domains of FN. The graph shows optical density (corresponding to number of bound receptors) vs. the different domains for 4 receptors

STEP 3 = > Use the relevant data to solve the question
Here, you must understand the concept of a synergistic effect, in other words, by adding another region which the receptor can bind to, you don't simply get twice as many receptors binding, but some greater multiple of the original binding. The correct answer is A. The $\alpha_5\beta_1$ (represented in black on the graph), shows binding to only domain 10 singly. However, when a fragment containing 9 and 10 are examined, the number of receptors binding increases almost 7 times, and then when 8, 9, and 10 are combined, it increases almost 20 times from only 10. The correct answer is A

Question 37

STEP 1= > What do you need to determine to solve the problem?
Key words are GPIIbIIIa, blood platelets, blood clot, connects platelets, and defect in V region

STEP 2 = > What relevant data provided in this problem is necessary in order to answer the question?
Again, examine the graph. The GPIIbIIIa is represented in white

STEP 3 = > Use the relevant data to solve the question
Here, you must determine the importance of the V region in binding to GPIIbIIIa. First, you should note that the GPIIbIIIa does not bind to the V region alone. In addition, GPIIb/IIIa binds equally to type III (12-14), type III (12-14, V), and type III (12-14, V, 15). This indicates that the V region has no binding sites for GPIIb/IIIa. Thus, the correct answer is C. A defect in the V region would have no effect on GPIIb/IIIa binding to FN.

Question 38

STEP 1 = > What do you need to determine to solve the problem?
The key words are all four ligands and affinity for type III (8-10)

STEP 2 = > What relevant data provided in this problem is necessary in order to answer the question?
Examining the graph, it is apparent that all four receptors do in fact bind with some affinity to type III (8-10)

STEP 3 = > Use the relevant data to solve the question
Examining the graph further, it should be noted that they indeed bind to type IIII (9-10) as well as type III (10), thus indicating that the important domain for the four molecules in type III (10). This domain in fact possesses the RGD peptide sequence that has been shown to bind with reasonable affinity to integrin receptors. Therefore, the correct answer is B.

UNIT 11

Questions 39–43

Question 39

STEP 1 = > What do you need to determine to solve the problem?
This is a straight forward question that asks you to apply the principles of physics to a biological system. It is asking you to "match" similar concepts.

STEP 2 = > What relevant data provided in this problem is necessary in order to answer the question?
Compare and equating the diagrams is what the question is asking. In the human jaw, the TMJ (temporomandibular joint) is the fulcrum, the muscles produce the effort and the teeth are the resistance.

STEP 3 = > Use the relevant data to solve the question
Equating all three parts and aligning them in correct order gives you a Class III lever system.

E↑(muscles of mastications   R↓(teeth)
F-TMJ

Answer C

Question 40

STEP 1 = > What do you need to determine to solve the problem?
This is another straight forward question asking you to identify which muscles produce the force to grind the food.

STEP 2 = > What relevant data provided in this problem is necessary in order to answer the question?
Draw a line in the general direction of the fibres of the muscle. You will find that most of the muscles travel in a near vertical direction. Remember the functions of a muscle from the summary given in the Guru Method Biology Manual (i.e. muscles contract and shorten to pull bones etc...).

STEP 3 = > Use the relevant data to solve the question
You will find that there are three muscles going in the same general direction, the masseter, the medial pterygoid and the temporalis.
Answer A.

Question 41

STEP 1 = > What do you need to determine to solve the problem?
This is one of the questions where you must use mathematics to figure out the solution as seen by the numbers and variables in the question.

STEP 2 = > What relevant data provided in this problem is necessary in order to answer the question?
Force at anterior teeth is x, distance of muscles from the fulcrum = 2cm, distance from fulcrum to the anterior teeth is 10cm.

STEP 3 = > Use the relevant data to solve the question
This is basic applied physics with levers using proportionality.

The force of the effort times its distance from the fulcrum equals the force of the resistance times its distance from the fulcrum.

force of muscle $\cdot$ 2 = x $\cdot$ 10
force of muscles = 5x

The answer is C

Question 42

STEP 1 = > What do you need to determine to solve the problem?
It is asking you to apply the concept of forces in levers again. Find out where the most force is being applied.

STEP 2 = > What relevant data provided in this problem is necessary in order to answer the question?
The system is a Class III lever system.

STEP 3 = > Use the relevant data to solve the question
Looking at the diagram the molars are closer to the point of force application. Since the system is a Class III lever there will be more force acting on the molars. Answer is B

Question 43

STEP 1 = > What do you need to determine to solve the problem?
This is another problem that requires applied mathematics. Find the distance from the
molars to the anterior teeth by utilizing the proportionalities.

STEP 2 = > What relevant data provided in this problem is necessary in order to answer
the question?

The point of application of the anterior teeth will be the 10cm the distance of the incisors
from the fulcrum because you can see that the incisors lie in the exact middle point of the
group of anterior teeth which means that the point of application of the force is 10cm by
symmetrical consideration.

STEP 3 = > Use the relevant data to solve the question

The muscles provide the power for the motion of the jaw and thereby generate Torque τ
around the fulcrum.

Let the point of application of the posterior teeth be equal to x.

In the question it is given that the force exerted by the posterior teeth is 4 times the force
exerted by the anterior teeth F.

Point of application of anterior teeth is 10 cm.

$\tau = 4F * x$
Also $\tau = F * 10$
Therefore we have
$$F*10 = 4F * x$$
$$x = 10/4 = 2.5 \text{ cm}$$

Now the approximate distance (D) between the anterior teeth and posterior teeth is just
the difference in the distance of points of application of forces exerted by the posterior and
anterior teeth from the fulcrum.
Therefore D = 10 - 2.5 = 7.5 cm

Note: The force is not applied at a particular point or points but is distributed throughout
the all the teeth in non-uniform way. But in order to do the calculation we assumed the
point of application of the anterior teeth at 10 cm using symmetric considerations.

Answer is A.

UNIT 12

Questions 44–45

Question 44

STEP 1 => What do you need to determine to solve the problem?
The key words are minimum dose and initial plasma concentration of 6.7×10^{-3} mg/L

STEP 2 => What relevant data provided in this problem is necessary in order to answer the question?
The passage has informed you that the *apparent volume* (V_D) into which a drug is distributed can be measured by the equation $V_D = d/C_0$ where d is the dosage of the drug and C_0 is the initial plasma concentration. In addition, as the question states that the patient is experiencing severe pain, it will be necessary for the drug to distribute through the entire body, thus $V_D \geq 15$ is needed for this case.

STEP 3 => Use the relevant data to solve the question
This now becomes a simple math problem, you know that C_0 is 6.7×10^{-3} mg/L, simply calculate V_D for the four answers. The correct answer is C. $V_D = 1.0 \times 10^{-1}$ mg/6.7×10^{-3} mg/L, so $V_D = 15$.

Question 45

STEP 1 => What do you need to determine to solve the problem?
You need to determine the clearance rate of morphine given the half-life.

STEP 2 => What relevant data provided in this problem is necessary in order to answer the question?
The question provides the formulas $Cl_p = V_D K_{el}$ where K_{el} is the rate of elimination. $K_{el} = 0.69/t_{1/2}$ where $t_{1/2}$ is the half-life of the drug. In addition, it says that the half-life of morphine is 2 hrs. Provided, you have calculated V_D correctly to be 15, this becomes a math problem

STEP 3 => Use the relevant data to solve the question
First, calculate $K_{el} = 0.69/2h = 0.345 h^{-1}$
Next, you can calculate the clearance $Cl_p = 15L (0.345 h^{-1}) = 5.2 L h^{-1}$
The correct answer is C.

UNIT 13

Questions 46–48

Question 46

STEP 1 = > What do you need to determine to solve the problem?
The key words are metabolic rate, elevated and feeding

STEP 2 = > What relevant data provided in this problem is necessary in order to answer the question?
The passage provides you with a graph of metabolic rate over time. In addition it tells you that the metabolic rate is measured by the volume of oxygen consumption. Within hours of swallowing prey, the python's metabolic rate begins to rise. The metabolic rate peaks at a rate of about 20 times the rate during fasting and then slowly decreases to fasting levels

STEP 3 = > Use the relevant data to solve the question
Simply examine the first graph. It shows that the MR begins to increase almost immediately following a feeding. It does not begin to level off until about 6 days after feeding and approached fasting levels by about 14 days on the graph. Therefore, the correct answer D.

Question 47

STEP 1 => What do you need to determine to solve the problem?
The key words are average blood flow and three days after feeding

STEP 2 = > What relevant data provided in this problem is necessary in order to answer the question?
The second set of graphs includes a graph showing blood flow over time. The graph shows that blood flow increases sharply right after feeding and peaks at about 36-48 hrs after feeding. It then begin to drop off slowly

STEP 3 = > Use the relevant data to solve the question
This question is simply a case of being able to read the graph. Note that time is in hrs, not days, so 3 days would be 72 hrs. Now, find the point on the blood flow graph at 72 hrs and draw a line horizontally to the left from that point. You will see that it intersects the y axis at about 30 ml kg^{-1} min^{-1}, so the correct answer is C.

Question 48

STEP 1 = > What do you need to determine to solve the problem?
The point of this question is that it wants you to correlate what you see in the graphs of
ventilation rate, heart rate, and blood flow with the metabolic rate graph. The key words are
peak at 48 hrs and advantage

STEP 2 = > What relevant data provided in this problem is necessary in order to answer
the question?
Examine all 4 graphs, note that the graphs of the heart rate, ventilation rate, and blood flow
all reach a maximum around 48 hrs, or 2 days. Next, looking at the graph of metabolic rate,
it also reaches a maximum somewhere around 2 days. From the passage, you know that the
metabolic rate is measured by the volume of oxygen consumption.

STEP 3 = > Use the relevant data to solve the question
Now, examining the answers, you should note that the correct answer involves a relationship
between the oxygen levels and the 4 physiological responses discussed. You should know
that blood carries oxygen, and the ventilation rate actually shows oxygen levels (oxygen
taken in). From the passage, you know that metabolic rate is related to oxygen consumption.
Since increases in ventilation rate, blood flow and heart rate all effectively deliver more
oxygen to the python's system, the python can consume more oxygen thereby increasing the
MR. As noted, all responses peak at about 2 days. Therefore the answer is A.

UNIT 14

Questions 49–51

Questions 49

STEP 1 = > What do you need to determine to solve the problem?
The key words are acidic nature and effect on efficacy of benzocaine

STEP 2 = > What relevant data provided in this problem is necessary in order to answer the question?
The passage states that the ionized form of LA is what blocks nerve transmission. It also states that they are weak bases. This concept is represented in the schematic which shows that the ionized form of the drug binds most strongly to inactivate the nerve channels, thereby suppressing pain

STEP 3 = > Use the relevant data to solve the question
From the diagram, the un-ionised form "B" is what penetrates the nerve and exerts its effect. In an acidic environment, weak bases are more highly ionized since the acidic environment will provide more H^+ to bind with the base. Thus, the acidic nature of a dental abscess would mean that there is less of the LA available in the "B" form.

This means that LA will be less effective since less penetration occurs. Therefore, the correct answer is B.

Question 50

STEP 1 = > What do you need to determine to solve the problem?
The key words are penetrate the maxillary artery and supplies part of the eye

STEP 2 = > What relevant data provided in this problem is necessary in order to answer the question?
The question states that sometimes during inferior alveolar nerve block, the needle can penetrate the maxillary artery

STEP 3 = > Use the relevant data to solve the question
Since the question also states that this artery is important for supplying the eye, an anesthetic introduced to this artery could result in blockage of nerve transmission to the eye. This would result in the eye being unable to function until the anesthetic wears off. Thus, the correct answer is D.

Question 51

<u>STEP 1 = > What do you need to determine to solve the problem?</u>
The key words are 2m tall person, steps on sharp object and feels pain 1 sec later

<u>STEP 2 = > What relevant data provided in this problem is necessary in order to answer the question?</u>
From the question, you know that the signal must travel from the foot to the brain.

<u>STEP 3 = > Use the relevant data to solve the question</u>
Since the person is 2m tall and it takes 1 second before the pain is registered, this means that it takes the signal approximately 1 second to travel the length of the body or about 2 m, thus signal is traveling at 2m/sec, or 200cm/sec, so the correct answer is D.

UNIT 15

Questions 52–56

Question 52

STEP 1 => What do you need to determine to solve the problem?
The key words are 35°C, rate of reaction of enzyme A and levels off

STEP 2 = > What relevant data provided in this problem is necessary in order to answer the question?
The passage states that enzymes act as biological catalysts that help speed up reactions by lowering the activation energy needed to bring reactants to their "transition state."

The reaction itself is often described by the following"
$E + S \rightarrow ES \rightarrow P + E$

It also provides graphs of 4 different enzymes. In the case of enzyme A, the graph shows that the enzyme can act through a temperature range of 0 to ~50°C

STEP 3 = > Use the relevant data to solve the question
Since 35°C is well within the temperature range which enzyme can act, a is incorrect. Since the rate of reaction levels off at this temperature, it indicates that there is a limiting factor in the reaction. In this case, once the substrate is completely saturated with the enzyme, there is no possibility of increasing the rate of reaction past this point. Thus, the correct answer is B.

Question 53

STEP 1 => What do you need to determine to solve the problem?
The key words are enzyme X and Y and true statement

STEP 2 = > What relevant data provided in this problem is necessary in order to answer the question?
Examine the graph of enzymes X and Y, it shows that X acts through a pH range of 0 to ~3.5 and Y acts through a range from ~5.5 to ~10

STEP 3 = > Use the relevant data to solve the question
Since the two enzymes act in completely different pH ranges with no overlap, it can be interpreted that they would not be able to act at the same place in the body at the same time, since a tissue will have a single pH at any point in time, the answer is A.

Question 54

STEP 1 = > What do you need to determine to solve the problem?
The key words are condition, change conformation and unable to bind to the substrate

STEP 2 = > What relevant data provided in this problem is necessary in order to answer the question?
Examining the graphs shows that A and B can act in certain temperature ranges and X and Y can act in certain pH ranges. Outside of these ranges, they are non-functional as their rate of reaction is 0.

STEP 3 = > Use the relevant data to solve the question
The correct answer is C, since enzyme x can only act in a range from about pH or 0-3.5. This pH is above this range

Question 55

STEP 1 = > What do you need to determine to solve the problem?
The key words are prevent enzyme Y and bringing substrate to its transition state

STEP 2 = > What relevant data provided in this problem is necessary in order to answer the question?
Again, examining the graph of enzyme Y, it shows that it acts in the range of about 5.5 to 10

STEP 3 = > Use the relevant data to solve the question
Thus, below pH 5.5, the rate of reaction for enzyme Y would be 0. Thus it would be unable to bring its substrate to the transition states, the correct answer is C.

Questions 56

STEP 1 => What do you need to determine to solve the problem?
The key words are enzymes X and Y and found in humans

STEP 2 = > What relevant data provided in this problem is necessary in order to answer the question?from the graphs, you know that enzyme x acts at low or very acidic pH, while enzyme Y acts at higher pH slightly acidic to highly basic.

STEP 3 = > Use the relevant data to solve the questionThis takes a bit of outside knowledge, but it is fairly common knowledge that the stomach is highly acidic. The pH of the body is generally neutral, or ~ 7, thus most tissues are only slightly lower or higher than this. Thus, the correct answer is C; the pH of the stomach is ~ 2, while that of the small intestine is ~ 6.

UNIT 16

Questions 57–60

Question 57

STEP 1 => What do you need to determine to solve the problem?
The key words are infect helper T-cells and body's defense system

STEP 2 = > What relevant data provided in this problem is necessary in order to answer the question?
The passage states that the immune response is part of the body's "specific defense system."

Two aspects of this defense mechanism are the primary and secondary immune responses. It also provides a graphical representation of the immune response over time demonstrating the cells involved in the different aspects of the immune response.

STEP 3 = > Use the relevant data to solve the question
Examination of the graph shows that T-cells are involved in both the primary and secondary immune response. Infection of the T-cells that prevents them from functioning properly would affect both responses, thus the answer is C.

Question 58

STEP 1 = > What do you need to determine to solve the problem?
The key words are when, secondary response peak and antigen B

STEP 2 = > What relevant data provided in this problem is necessary in order to answer the question?
Again, examine the graph. It shows a primary and secondary response to antigen A. The peak primary response occurs about 10-12 days, and the peak secondary response occurs about 40-42 days after exposure.

STEP 3 = > Use the relevant data to solve the question
This reflected a 30-days lapse between a primary and secondary immune response. Now, noting that the primary immune response for antigen B occurs at about 38-40 days, a secondary response is likely at around 68-70 days, the answer D.

Question 59

STEP 1 = > What do you need to determine to solve the problem?
The key words are severe allergy and administered a second time

STEP 2 = > What relevant data provided in this problem is necessary in order to answer the question?
Examining the graph, it shows that once the secondary response occurs, the number of antibodies to the antigen increase drastically.

STEP 3 = > Use the relevant data to solve the question
Such a drastic increase in the amount of antibodies present would greatly affect the degree of the reaction to the antigen, in this case ampicillin. Therefore, the correct answer is A.

Question 60

STEP 1 = > What do you need to determine to solve the problem?
The key words are how many more antibodies and secondary compared to primary

STEP 2 = > What relevant data provided in this problem is necessary in order to answer the question?
Examining the graph, it shows that the primary immune response peaks at about 10^1 antibodies, while the secondary immune response peaks at about 10^4.

STEP 3 = > Use the relevant data to solve the question
This means that the secondary immune response produce 1000x's the number of antibodies than the primary immune response. The answer is C.

UNIT 17

Questions 61–64

Question 61

STEP 1 = > What do you need to determine to solve the problem?
The key words are true statement and experiment 1

STEP 2 = > What relevant data provided in this problem is necessary in order to answer the question?
First examine the 4 statements. Then looking back at the passage, experiment 1 involves 2 plates divided in half, with half of plate A treated with UV radiation, and half of plate B treated with green light. You are also shown the number of colonies present on each side of the dishes after treatment

STEP 3 = > Use the relevant data to solve the question
The results show that after radiation treatment, 10 colonies are present, but the untreated sides of the dishes and the green light-treated dishes all showed 30 colonies. Thus, the correct answer is B.

Question 62

STEP 1 = > What do you need to determine to solve the problem?
The key words are comparing dish A from both experiments

STEP 2 = > What relevant data provided in this problem is necessary in order to answer the question?
Again, examine the chart showing bacterial colony growth following the different treatments for experiment 1 and experiment 2. Note that the more colonies are present on side 1 of dish A in experiment 2 than experiment 1. This number is still less than the number present for the untreated and green light-treated samples.

STEP 3 = > Use the relevant data to solve the question
The only difference between the two experiments is that the plates in experiment 2 are exposed to incandescent light after UV, green light, or no treatment. Since, this seems to result in a significant increase in the number of bacterial colonies on side 1 of dish A, it indicates that incandescent light exposure helps repair the effects of UV damage. The answer is C.

Question 63

STEP 1 = > What do you need to determine to solve the problem?
The key words are glass lid and not removed prior to experiment

STEP 2 = > What relevant data provided in this problem is necessary in order to answer the question?
In this case, when the glass lid is not removed, the number of bacterial colonies on side 1 of dish A is not significantly different from the untreated and green-lighted treated samples, even when the lid is removed.

STEP 3 = > Use the relevant data to solve the question
These results indicate that the glass blocks the UV radiation since there is no reduction in colony number when the glass is left in place and exposed to UV radiation. There is a significant reduction in colony number when the glass is removed and the bacteria exposed to UV radiation. Thus, the answer is A.

Question 64

STEP 1 = > What do you need to determine to solve the problem?
The key word is control

STEP 2 = > What relevant data provided in this problem is necessary in order to answer the question?
The passage states that side 2 of both plates is left untreated

STEP 3 = > Use the relevant data to solve the question
The correct answer D. The control sample in these experiments would be one in which the sample is prepared and treated in the same way as the test sample, except no treatment is administered to the sample. Since the plates are divided in half and only one side is treated, the untreated side constitutes a control.

UNIT 18

Questions 65–69

Question 65

STEP 1 = > What do you need to determine to solve the problem?
The question requires you to calculate the probability of a certain genetic outcome.
To do so, you must understand how heredity works.

STEP 2 = > What relevant data provided in this problem is necessary in order to answer the question?
The passage indicates that each parent passes along a random allele, and that the phenotype of the offspring depends on its genotype and its dominant/recessive character.

STEP 3 = > Use the relevant data to solve the question
The Punnett square for two heterozygous parents shows four possible genotypes: TT, Tt, Tt, and tt.
Two of the four are heterozygous, and since inheritance of alleles is random, any offspring has a 2/4 or 50% chance of being heterozygous.

Question 66

STEP 1 = > What do you need to determine to solve the problem?
The question requires you to identify the genotype that corresponds to the given phenotype.
To do so, you must determine the effect of genotype on phenotype for the given traits.

STEP 2 = > What relevant data provided in this problem is necessary in order to answer the question?
The passage indicates that dominant traits are expressed whenever one or more dominant alleles are present, and that recessive traits only appear in homozygous recessive individuals.

STEP 3 = > Use the relevant data to solve the question
Tall and yellow are both dominant traits, so any genotype including T and Y can be tall and yellow.
However, wrinkled is recessive and requires a genotype of rr. Therefore, only Choice C can yield the given phenotype.

Question 67

STEP 1 = > What do you need to determine to solve the problem?
The question requires you to calculate the phenotypic ratio of the offspring of two doubly heterozygous pea plants.
To do so, you must apply statistics to the peas.

STEP 2 = > What relevant data provided in this problem is necessary in order to answer the question?
The passage indicates that the two traits are independent and follow normal inheritance patterns including dominance.

STEP 3 = > Use the relevant data to solve the question
The phenotype ratio in each trait is 3:1.
Each trait is independent of the other, so the ratio of tall to short plants is 3:1 in both the green and yellow populations, and vice versa. The phenotype ratios for the population with respect to both traits can be calculated by multiplying the individual ratios together. 3 x 3 = 9, 3 x 1 = 3, 1 x 3 = 3, and 1 x 1 = 1; so 3:1 x 3:1 = 9:3:3:1, with 9 tall yellow plants, 3 short yellow, 3 tall green, and 1 short green in an ideal group of 16.

Question 68

STEP 1 = > What do you need to determine to solve the problem?
The question requires you to identify the phenotype of the given pea plant.
To do so, you must determine what effect each allele will have on phenotype.

STEP 2 = > What relevant data provided in this problem is necessary in order to answer the question?
The passage indicates that any dominant allele will manifest in the phenotype, while only homozygous recessives are exhibited.

STEP 3 = > Use the relevant data to solve the question
The genotype tt is homozygous recessive and codes for short, while Yy and Rr are heterozygous and code for yellow and round, respectively. Therefore, the pea plant is short with round yellow peas.

Question 69

STEP 1 = > What do you need to determine to solve the problem?
The question requires you to identify the parents most likely to produce completely heterozygous offspring.

STEP 2 = > What relevant data provided in this problem is necessary in order to answer the question?
The passage indicates that each parent randomly passes one of its alleles down to an offspring, and that the genes for all three traits assort independently.

STEP 3 = > Use the relevant data to solve the question
All of the given parent pairs have some chance of producing completely heterozygous offspring, but pairs that are homozygous for all traits, with one plant dominant and one recessive for each trait, have a 100% chance of producing heterozygous offspring. TTrrYY and ttRRyy parents will produce heterozygous offspring every time.

UNIT 19

Questions 70-74

Question 70

STEP 1 = > What do you need to determine to solve the problem?
The question requires you to identify the chromosome responsible for Down Syndrome.
To do so, you must find the defective chromosome.

STEP 2 = > What relevant data provided in this problem is necessary in order to answer the question?
The passage indicates that genetic disorders are caused by defects in genes or chromosomes.

STEP 3 = > Use the relevant data to solve the question
All of the chromosomes appear normal except chromosome 21.
There are three copies of the chromosome instead of two, a condition known as trisomy that makes Chromosome 21 responsible for Down Syndrome.

Question 71

STEP 1 = > What do you need to determine to solve the problem?
The question requires you to identify the mode of inheritance of Tay-Sachs disease.
To do so, you must read the family tree.

STEP 2 = > What relevant data provided in this problem is necessary in order to answer the question?
The passage indicates that sex-linked disorders are characterized by an uneven distribution between the sexes of those afflicted.
Also, most genetic disease follows the classic Mendelian dominance pattern.

STEP 3 = > Use the relevant data to solve the question
In the family tree, there are an equal number of afflicted and carrier individuals of each sex, so the disease is autosomal and not sex-linked.
Also, for a disorder to have carriers, it must be recessive. If it was dominant, everyone with even a single copy of the gene would have the disease. Therefore, Tay-Sachs disease is autosomal recessive.

Question 72

STEP 1 = > What do you need to determine to solve the problem?
The question requires you to identify the mode of inheritance of Huntington's disease.
To do so, you must understand how genetic diseases are inherited.

STEP 2 = > What relevant data provided in this problem is necessary in order to answer the question?
The passage indicates that sex-linked disorders are characterized by an uneven distribution between the sexes of those afflicted.
Also, most genetic disease follows the classic Mendelian dominance pattern.

STEP 3 = > Use the relevant data to solve the question
Since the disease is known to affect both men and women equally, it must be autosomal and not sex-linked.
However, since every single child of a parent with the disease has at least a 50% chance of inheriting it, and there is no mention of carriers, the disease must be dominant. If it was recessive, an individual with Huntington's would not be as likely to have afflicted children. Therefore, Huntington's disease is an autosomal dominant disorder.

Question 73

STEP 1 = > What do you need to determine to solve the problem?
The question requires you to calculate the probability of the offspring of the given parents having hemophilia.
To do so, you must model the inheritance of the disease.

STEP 2 = > What relevant data provided in this problem is necessary in order to answer the question?
The passage indicates that X-linked diseases are more likely to affect men than women, and that recessive diseases require two recessive alleles in order to afflict an individual.

STEP 3 = > Use the relevant data to solve the question
The probability for both sexes is actually the same, as the father only determines the sex and does not alter the equation for hemophilia in this case.
He cannot pass on his defective X chromosome onto a son, whose only chance to have the disease comes from his mother, and even a daughter, who will receive that defect, still will not manifest the disease unless she inherits it from her mother as well. Therefore, the probability for both sexes is 50%.

Question 74

STEP 1 = > What do you need to determine to solve the problem?
The question requires you to identify the source of a genetic defect.
To do so, you must understand the differences between the types of genetic material.

STEP 2 = > What relevant data provided in this problem is necessary in order to answer the question?
The passage indicates that genetic disorders are caused by defective genes or chromosomes.

STEP 3 = > Use the relevant data to solve the question
RNA cannot pass on a genetic defect; only DNA can.
Because children can only inherit the defect from their mothers, not their fathers, the disorder clearly does not obey the rules of nuclear DNA inheritance. Rather, the defect must be in the mitochondrial DNA, which is only inherited from the mother.

UNIT 20

Questions 75-79

Question 75

STEP 1 = > What do you need to determine to solve the problem?
The question requires you to identify the DNA complement of the given strand.
To do so, you must understand the interactions of DNA.

STEP 2 = > What relevant data provided in this problem is necessary in order to answer the question?
The passage indicates that DNA strands bind to each other in C-G and A-T pairs, in opposite 5'-3'orientations.

STEP 3 = > Use the relevant data to solve the question
The DNA complement for the given strand must have all the complementary bases to the strand in question, but they must be in reverse 5'-3' order compared to the template.
Therefore, only B has the proper sequence and orientation.

Question 76

STEP 1 = > What do you need to determine to solve the problem?
The question requires you to identify the RNA synthesized from the DNA complement of the given strand.
To do so, you must understand the interactions of DNA and RNA.

STEP 2 = > What relevant data provided in this problem is necessary in order to answer the question?
The passage indicates that DNA strands bind to each other in C-G and A-T pairs, in opposite 5'-3'orientations.
RNA is synthesized from DNA in a similar way, except using U in place of T.

STEP 3 = > Use the relevant data to solve the question
Since the complement bases of a set of complement bases are identical to the bases of the original template and in the same order, the RNA strand synthesized from the complement of the DNA strand given must have the same sequence as the given DNA, with the sole exception of U in place of T.
Therefore, D is the correct RNA strand.

Question 77

STEP 1 = > What do you need to determine to solve the problem?
The question requires you to calculate the percentage of a certain base in a DNA sample.
To do so, you must understand the composition of DNA.

STEP 2 = > What relevant data provided in this problem is necessary in order to answer the question?
The passage indicates that DNA is typically held in a two-stranded double helix by complementary bases.

STEP 3 = > Use the relevant data to solve the question
The percentages of A and T and those of G and C must be identical in double-stranded DNA.
20% G means that there must also be 20% C. 20 + 20 = 40, meaning that A and T must comprise 100 − 40 = 60% of the bases. Since the amounts of A and T must be equal, the percentage of T in the DNA must be 60/2 = 30%.

Question 78

STEP 1 = > What do you need to determine to solve the problem?
The question requires you to identify the elements involved in hydrogen bonding. To do so, you must understand the structure of the bases and the chemistry behind hydrogen bonding.

STEP 2 = > What relevant data provided in this problem is necessary in order to answer the question?
The passage indicates that the bases are held together in the double helix by hydrogen bonds.

STEP 3 = > Use the relevant data to solve the question
The two primary elements that participate in hydrogen bonding are oxygen and nitrogen.

Question 79

STEP 1 = > What do you need to determine to solve the problem?
The question requires you to determine the nature of nucleic acid.
To do so, you must understand the structure of each type.

STEP 2 = > What relevant data provided in this problem is necessary in order to answer the question?
The passage indicates that DNA contains thymine, while RNA contains uracil.

STEP 3 = > Use the relevant data to solve the question
The inequality between complementary base pair percentages indicates that the sample is single-stranded, while the presence of uracil means that it is RNA.

UNIT 21

Questions 80-84

Question 80

STEP 1 = > What do you need to determine to solve the problem?
The question requires you to identify the function dependent on calcium.
To do so, you must know the physiological role of calcium.

STEP 2 = > What relevant data provided in this problem is necessary in order to answer the question?
The passage indicates that calcitonin and PTH keep blood calcium levels in the range necessary for physiological function.

STEP 3 = > Use the relevant data to solve the question
Calcium is crucial in the muscles, especially the heart, because of its role in turning an action potential into a contraction stimulus.

Question 81

STEP 1 = > What do you need to determine to solve the problem?
The question requires you to determine the clinical result of a parathyroid tumor.
To do so, you must understand the effect of PTH.

STEP 2 = > What relevant data provided in this problem is necessary in order to answer the question?
The passage indicates that PTH is responsible for increasing blood calcium levels by stimulating bone resorption.

STEP 3 = > Use the relevant data to solve the question
A hormone-secreting parathyroid tumor would elevate PTH levels, causing bone mass to decrease as it tries to raise the blood calcium level.

Question 82

STEP 1 = > What do you need to determine to solve the problem?
The question requires you to determine the response to hypocalcemia.
To do so, you must understand the roles of calcitonin and PTH in blood calcium regulation.

STEP 2 = > What relevant data provided in this problem is necessary in order to answer the question?
The passage indicates that PTH is responsible for increasing blood calcium levels by stimulating bone resorption, while calcitonin reduces blood calcium by stimulating bone deposit.

STEP 3 = > Use the relevant data to solve the question
Hypocalcemia, a condition, of low blood calcium, would stimulate the production of PTH and suppress calcitonin in order to elevate the level of calcium.

Question 83

STEP 1 = > What do you need to determine to solve the problem?
The question requires you to identify the cell stimulated by calcitonin. To do so, you must understand the function of calcitonin.

STEP 2 = > What relevant data provided in this problem is necessary in order to answer the question?
The passage indicates that calcitonin lowers blood calcium levels by stimulating bone deposit.

STEP 3 = > Use the relevant data to solve the question
Calcitonin must stimulate the cells responsible for continued bone growth, osteoblasts. Osteoclasts are responsible for bone resorption and are stimulated by PTH, while osteocytes are mature bone cell that do not actively deposit or break down bone matrix, and osteoprogenitor cells are the precursor tissue of other bone cells.

Question 84

STEP 1 = > What do you need to determine to solve the problem?
The question requires you to identify the systems most relevant to the action of calcitonin and PTH. To do so, you must understand the roles of calcitonin and PTH in blood calcium regulation.

STEP 2 = > What relevant data provided in this problem is necessary in order to answer the question?
The passage indicates that calcitonin and PTH keep blood calcium levels in the range necessary for physiological function.

STEP 3 = > Use the relevant data to solve the question
Since PTH and calcitonin are hormones that travel through the bloodstream and regulate blood chemistry, the endocrine and circulatory systems are the most closely tied into the hormones' function.

UNIT 22

Questions 85-89

Question 85

STEP 1 = > What do you need to determine to solve the problem?
The question requires you to trace the route of blood through the heart, beginning at the lungs.
To do so, you must identify the four chambers of the heart.

STEP 2 = > What relevant data provided in this problem is necessary in order to answer the question?
The passage indicates that the diagram shows the heart from an anterior view, and that blood entering the heart first enters an atrium, then a ventricle.

STEP 3 = > Use the relevant data to solve the question
According to the diagram, blood returns from the lungs to the left atrium, goes to the left ventricle and then to the body; when it returns, it enters the right atrium before being pumped into the right ventricle and back to the lungs.

Question 86

STEP 1 = > What do you need to determine to solve the problem?
The question requires you to identify the false statement.
To do so, you must determine which of the statements are true.

STEP 2 = > What relevant data provided in this problem is necessary in order to answer the question?
The passage indicates that arteries carry blood away from the heart and veins carry blood back to it.

STEP 3 = > Use the relevant data to solve the question
Not all arteries carry oxygenated blood and not all veins carry deoxygenated blood.
The majority do, including all those leading away from the left ventricle and to the right atrium. However, the oxygenation in the pulmonary circuit is reversed, with the pulmonary artery carrying deoxygenated blood and the pulmonary vein carrying freshly oxygenated blood.

Question 87

STEP 1 = > What do you need to determine to solve the problem?
The question requires you to identify the blood vessel attached to the right atrium.
To do so, you must determine what function the right atrium serves.

STEP 2 = > What relevant data provided in this problem is necessary in order to answer the question?
The passage indicates that blood enters an atrium first on entering the heart.

STEP 3 = > Use the relevant data to solve the question
The right atrium receives blood from the body, through the vessel known as the vena cava.
Blood exits the right ventricle into the pulmonary artery, is returned to the left atrium via the pulmonary vein, and is pumped by the left ventricle into the aorta and back to the body.

Question 88

STEP 1 = > What do you need to determine to solve the problem?
The question requires you to identify the highest-pressure chamber of the heart.
To do so, you must determine the unique function of each chamber.

STEP 2 = > What relevant data provided in this problem is necessary in order to answer the question?
The passage indicates that the ventricles pump blood away from the heart to the body and lungs.

STEP 3 = > Use the relevant data to solve the question
The left ventricle is responsible for pumping blood through the high-pressure artery system to the entire body, leading it to have the highest pressure of any heart chamber.
It also has thicker walls, because it has to work harder to pump blood to the body.

Question 89

STEP 1 = > What do you need to determine to solve the problem?
The question requires you to identify the fetal adaptation that bypasses the liver. To do so, you must understand the unique features of the fetal circulatory system.

STEP 2 = > What relevant data provided in this problem is necessary in order to answer the question?
The passage indicates that blood passes through the liver while returning to the heart.

STEP 3 = > Use the relevant data to solve the question
The body's blood is sent to the liver by the hepatic portal vein, which is bypassed during pregnancy by the ductus venosus.
The placenta is the blood interface between mother and child, while the foramen ovale and ductus arteriosus are fetal heart adaptations that bypass the pulmonary circuit.

UNIT 23

Questions 90-94

Question 90

STEP 1 = > What do you need to determine to solve the problem?
The question requires you to identify the growth curve in the diagram.
To do so, you must understand the types of population growth.

STEP 2 = > What relevant data provided in this problem is necessary in order to answer the question?
The passage indicates that population growth is subjected to competitive and environmental constraints.

STEP 3 = > Use the relevant data to solve the question
The type of growth shown in the diagram, with a period of initial exponential growth followed by a leveling off and stabilization of population size is logistic growth.

Question 91

STEP 1 = > What do you need to determine to solve the problem?
The question requires you to correctly arrange the population growth equation.
To do so, you must determine which factors add to and subtract from the population.

STEP 2 = > What relevant data provided in this problem is necessary in order to answer the question?
The passage indicates that both births/deaths and movement in and out of the population contribute to population change.

STEP 3 = > Use the relevant data to solve the question
Births and immigration both add individuals to the population, while deaths and emigration take them away; therefore Choice D has the correct arrangement for the equation.

Question 92

STEP 1 = > What do you need to determine to solve the problem?
The question requires you to identify the species interaction between ants and aphids. To do so, you must understand how species interact and affect each other.

STEP 2 = > What relevant data provided in this problem is necessary in order to answer the question?
The passage indicates that species interactions, described by population ecology, can have drastic effects on population size and viability.

STEP 3 = > Use the relevant data to solve the question
Since aphids supply ants with food in return for protection and care, both populations are greatly stabilized and their carrying capacities are increased. This interaction, benefiting both species, is known as mutualism.

Question 93

STEP 1 = > What do you need to determine to solve the problem?
The question requires you to calculate the amount of the population that carries the genetic disease described. To do so, you must use the Hardy-Weinberg equilibrium.

STEP 2 = > What relevant data provided in this problem is necessary in order to answer the question?
The passage indicates that the frequencies of alleles p and q in a population must total 1, as must the frequencies of the genotypes pp, pq, and qq.

STEP 3 = > Use the relevant data to solve the question
The disease affects the 4% of the population that is homozygous recessive, or q^2. Therefore, q = $\sqrt{0.04}$ = 0.2. Since $p + q = 1$, $p = 1 - q = 0.8$. The Hardy-Weinberg equation $p^2 + 2pq + q^2 = 1$ must accordingly be structured as $0.8^2 + 2 \times 0.8 \times 0.2 + 0.2^2 = 0.64 + 0.32 + 0.04 = 1$. In a recessive disease, the carriers are the heterozygous population, in this case represented by $2pq$ = 0.32 and comprising 32% of the population.

Question 94

STEP 1 = > What do you need to determine to solve the problem?
The question requires you to calculate the effective population size of a given population. To do so, you must apply the uneven sex-ratio equation.

STEP 2 = > What relevant data provided in this problem is necessary in order to answer the question?
The passage indicates that the effective population size N_e can be calculated using the formula $N_e = (4 \times M \times F)/(M + F)$, where M and F are the numbers of male and female individuals.

STEP 3 = > Use the relevant data to solve the question
Since 30 of the 100 individuals are male, the other 70 are female. Therefore, the effective population size is $N_e = (4 \times 30 \times 70)/(30 + 70) = 8400/100 = 84$.

Solutions: **General Chemistry**

UNIT 1

Questions 1–4

Question 1

STEP 1 = > What do you need to determine to solve the problem?
Which statement is true regarding $\Delta G°$ being less than zero

STEP 2 = > What relevant data provided in this problem is necessary in order to answer the question?
The passage provides you with a description of free energy and tells you that the relationship between reaction spontaneity, entropy and enthalpy is given by the Gibbs free energy function:
$\Delta G = \Delta H - T \Delta S$

The change in the free energy of a system under standard state conditions is called the standard state free energy of reaction ($\Delta G°$)

$\Delta G° = \Delta H° - T\Delta S°$

In addition, it also provides you with the following information regarding the favorability of a process

Favourable	Unfavourable
$\Delta H° < 0$	$\Delta H° > 0$
$\Delta S° > 0$	$\Delta S° < 0$

STEP 3 = > Use the relevant data to solve the question
From the above table, negative enthalpy and positive entropy indicate a favourable process. When these sign conventions were placed into the Gibbs free energy equation, it is apparent that when both enthalpy and entropy are favourable, ΔG will be negative. Therefore, a negative ΔG indicates a spontaneous process. The answer is B.

Question 2

<u>STEP 1 = > What do you need to determine to solve the problem?</u>
What is the effect of increasing temperature on ΔG

<u>STEP 2 = > What relevant data provided in this problem is necessary in order to answer the question?</u>
The passage provides you with the following equation for ΔG.
$\Delta G = \Delta H - T \Delta S$
In addition, the question gives you that
$\Delta H = 200$ kJ/mol and $\Delta S = 800$ J/(mol-K).

<u>STEP 3 = > Use the relevant data to solve the question</u>
Both ΔH and ΔS are positive in this circumstance. Therefore, as T increases, the TΔS term becomes larger and therefore, $\Delta H - T\Delta S$ will become smaller. This means that over a large range of T, the reaction will go from a positive ΔG at lower T to a negative ΔG at high temperature. Given that a negative ΔG indicates a spontaneous process (see question 1), and that an increase in T causes ΔG to become more negative, the answer is A.

Question 3

<u>STEP 1 = > What do you need to determine to solve the problem?</u>
You need to calculate the free energy of the given reaction at 25°C

<u>STEP 2 = > What relevant data provided in this problem is necessary in order to answer the question?</u>
The passage provides you with the following equation for ΔG.
$\Delta G = \Delta H - T \Delta S$
In addition, you are given a table with the ΔH and ΔS values for the various chemical species in the reaction

<u>STEP 3 = > Use the relevant data to solve the question</u>
First you need to calculate ΔH and ΔS for the overall reaction. $\Delta H = \Delta H$ (products) - ΔH (reactants) (the same applies for ΔS). So
$\Delta H = 2(-90.79) - (2(0) + (0))$
$\Delta H = -181.58$ kJ/mol
$\Delta S = 2(70.7) - (2(76.027) + (205.0))$
$\Delta S = -215.654$ J/(mol·K)
$\Delta G = -181.58$ kJ/mol $- (298K)(-0.215654$ kJ/(mol·K)
$\Delta G = -117.3$ kJ – answer A.

Question 4

STEP 1 = > What do you need to determine to solve the problem?
Which process would not result in a positive change in entropy

STEP 2 = > What relevant data provided in this problem is necessary in order to answer the question?
Entropy can be defined as disorder within a system. $\Delta S = \Delta S$ (products) - ΔS (reactants), so an increase in disorder would result in a positive entropy change

STEP 3 = > Use the relevant data to solve the question
If an increase in disorder would result in a positive change in entropy, then simply examine the statements and see which would not be an increase in disorder. Answer A is an increase in disorder because one molecule is being split into two (two is greater than one, therefore more disorder). Answer B is an increase in disorder because more gas is being created during the reaction; this means that there will be more molecules and therefore more disorder. Answer C is an increase in disorder because the molecules of a liquid are in a much more ordered state than those of a gas. The answer is D, this is because just as with the previous statement, the molecules in a solid are much more ordered than those in a liquid (this is why a liquid can flow and a solid can't), and therefore, when changing from a liquid to a solid, the system must become more ordered.

UNIT 2

Questions 5-8

Question 5

STEP 1 = > What do you need to determine to solve the problem?
When is the reaction always spontaneous

STEP 2 = > What relevant data provided in this problem is necessary in order to answer the question?
The passage provides you with a description of free energy and tells you that the relationship between reaction spontaneity, entropy and enthalpy is given by the Gibbs free energy function:
$\Delta G = \Delta H - T \Delta S$

You are also given a table with different signs for ΔH and ΔS
You are also told that a negative ΔG means that the reaction is spontaneous.

STEP 3 = > Use the relevant data to solve the question
Given the equation, you want to know when ΔG would always be negative. Since T is in K, there is no possibility of having a negative T. So, if ΔH is negative and ΔS is positive, the end result will always be a negative ΔG, the answer is B or the first row "A".

Question 6

STEP 1 = > What do you need to determine to solve the problem?
When the reaction would be spontaneous only at high T

STEP 2 = > What relevant data provided in this problem is necessary in order to answer the question?
The passage provides you with a description of free energy and tells you that the relationship between reaction spontaneity, entropy and enthalpy is given by the Gibbs free energy function:
$\Delta G = \Delta H - T \Delta S$
You are also given a table with different signs for ΔH and ΔS
You are also told that a negative ΔG means that the reaction is spontaneous.

STEP 3 = > Use the relevant data to solve the question
Now, you are looking for what happens with increasing T to ΔG. If both ΔH and ΔS are positive, and the T was close to zero, ΔG would be positive because subtracting the TΔS term would not be enough to overcome the positive ΔH term. However, as T increased, the TΔS term would become more significant and would outweigh the positive ΔH term above a certain T, so the answer is **A** or "C" in the 3ʳᵈ row.

Question 7

STEP 1 = > What do you need to determine to solve the problem?
The free energy of the reaction

STEP 2 = > What relevant data provided in this problem is necessary in order to answer the question?
The passage provides you with a description of free energy and tells you that the relationship between reaction spontaneity, entropy and enthalpy is given by the Gibbs free energy function:
$\Delta G = \Delta H - T \Delta S$
You are also given the values of ΔH and ΔS and told that told that the reaction is performed under NTP.

STEP 3 = > Use the relevant data to solve the question
You must recall that NTP(normal temperature and pressure) means 20°C and 1 atm. So, converting T to Kelvin, T = 273 + 20 = 293 K

Given that ΔH = -181.57 kJ/mol and ΔS = 200 J/mol·K;
$\Delta G = -181.57 + 293 (0.200) = -181.57 - 58.6$
$\Delta G = -240.17$ kJ; answer B

Question 8

STEP 1 = > <u>What do you need to determine to solve the problem?</u>
If you have a negative enthalpy and negative entropy, how would T affect ΔG

STEP 2 = > <u>What relevant data provided in this problem is necessary in order to answer</u>
<u>the question?</u>
The passage provides you with a description of free energy and tells you that the relationship between reaction spontaneity, entropy and enthalpy is given by the Gibbs free energy function:
$\Delta G = \Delta H - T \Delta S$
You are also given a table with different signs for ΔH and ΔS
You are also told that a negative ΔG means that the reaction is spontaneous.

STEP 3 = > <u>Use the relevant data to solve the question</u>
If both terms were negative, ΔH would have to be much greater than $T \Delta S$ in order for ΔG to be negative. As T increases, $T \Delta S$ will become larger so eventually it will be greater than ΔH making ΔG positive so the reaction non-spontaneous. The opposite would happen at low T. So the answer is C.

UNIT 3

Question 9-11

Question 9

STEP 1 = > What do you need to determine to solve the problem?
Which of the metals listed can be obtained from an aqueous solution

STEP 2 = > What relevant data provided in this problem is necessary in order to answer the question?
You are given the reduction potentials of the three metals and the reduction potentials of water under both acidic and basic conditions

STEP 3 = > Use the relevant data to solve the question
Simply examine the reduction potentials given. It is immediately apparent that the reduction potentials of all three metals is much more negative than that of water under both acidic and basic conditions. In order to produce the metal, it is necessary for it to be the most readily reduced species within the system. Therefore, the answer is D; none can be obtained from aqueous solution.

Question 10

STEP 1 = > What do you need to determine to solve the problem?
Which equation corresponds to the anode of the Down's cell.

STEP 2 = > What relevant data provided in this problem is necessary in order to answer the question?
You are told that the Down's cell is an industrial electrolytic cell that produces metallic sodium metal from molten Sodium Chloride. Chlorine gas is formed as a by-product of the process. You are also given the reduction equations for Na and Cl

STEP 3 = > Use the relevant data to solve the question
You must recall that oxidation occurs at the anode. The question has provided the reduction equations. Oxidation is the loss of electrons while reduction is the gain of electrons. Since you know that you are splitting NaCl into Na (s) and Cl_2 (g) during this process as stated in the passage, this means that Na^+ must gain electrons in order to form Na (s), while Cl^- must lose electrons to form Cl_2 (g). Therefore, Cl^- is being oxidized and would therefore represent the cathode. Thus, the answer is C.

Question 11

STEP 1 = > <u>What do you need to determine to solve the problem?</u>
The EMF that must be applied for the formation of Na (s)

STEP 2 = > <u>What relevant data provided in this problem is necessary in order to answer</u>
<u>the question?</u>
You are given the reduction potentials for Na^+ and Cl_2 (g).

$Na^+(aq) + e^- \rightarrow Na(s)$ $E° = -2.71$ V

$Cl_2(g) + 2e^- \rightarrow 2Cl^-$ $E° = 1.36$ V

STEP 3 = > <u>Use the relevant data to solve the question</u>
As the reduction potential of the second half reaction is greater than the first half cell
reaction, so the second half reaction is a reduction half reaction, while the first half reaction
is an oxidation half reaction.

Reduction half cell reaction

$Cl_2(g) + 2e^- \rightarrow 2Cl^-$ $E° = 1.36$ V   (at cathode)

Oxidation half cell reaction

$Na(s) \rightarrow Na^+(aq) + e^-$ $E° = 2.71$ V   (at anode)

To obtain the cell reaction, multiply the oxidation half reaction by factor 2 so that when
the half reactions are added together, the electrons cancel. This does not affect the half cell
potentials.

$2\,Na(s) \rightarrow 2Na^+(aq) + 2e^-$ $E° = 2.71$ V

$Cl_2(g) + 2e^- \rightarrow 2Cl^-$ $E° = 1.36$ V

$2\,Na(s) + Cl_2(g) \rightarrow 2Na^+(aq) + 2Cl^-$ $E°$ cell

We can calculate the cell emf using the equation

$E°_{cell} = E°_{cathode} - E°_{anode}$
$E°_{cell} = 1.36$ V $- (-2.71)$
$E°_{cell} = 4.07$ V

Answer C.

UNIT 4

Questions 12-14

Question 12

STEP 1 = > What do you need to determine to solve the problem?
How many grams of Al are produced

STEP 2 = > What relevant data provided in this problem is necessary in order to answer the question?
You are told that the relationship between the amount of substance formed at an electrode is directly proportional to the amount of current passed through the solution. It also states that the proportionality constant is the gram equivalent weight of the substance. You are also told that 1 Coulomb = 1 amp-s; 1 Faraday = 96500 coulombs = 1 mole of e⁻ You are also given the mw of Al

STEP 3 = > Use the relevant data to solve the question
So, what is being stated is that the grams formed = current passed x GEW. You must write the equation for the reduction of Al, which in this case is as follows
$Al^+ + 3e^- \rightarrow Al$

So, (31500 C) (1 mole e⁻/96500 C) (1 mole Al/3 mole e⁻) (27g Al/ 1 mole Al) = 2.9g, answer is D.

Helpful hint: Always remember to make sure all of the units are cancelled out during the multiplication such that your answer has the proper units.

Question 13

STEP 1 = > What do you need to determine to solve the problem?
How many grams of Cl_2 gas are formed

STEP 2 = > What relevant data provided in this problem is necessary in order to answer the question?
You are told that the relationship between the amount of substance formed at an electrode is directly proportional to the amount of current passed through the solution. It also states that the proportionality constant is the gram equivalent weight of the substance. You are also told that 1 Coulomb = 1 amp-s; 1 Faraday = 96500 coulombs = 1 mole of e⁻ You are also given the mw of Li

STEP 3 = > Use the relevant data to solve the question
So once again, we must write the equation, this time for the reduction of Li.
$Li^+ + e^- \rightarrow Li$
So, (10g Li) (1 mol Li/ 6.9 g Li) (1 mol e⁻/ 1 mol Li) (96500 C/ 1 mol e⁻) = 139855.07 C
Since 1 C = 1 amp-s; 139855.07 C/2400 s = 58.3 amp, the answer is C.

Question 14

STEP 1 = > What do you need to determine to solve the problem?
How many amps must be passed through LiCl to produce 10 g of Li after 40 mins

STEP 2 = > What relevant data provided in this problem is necessary in order to answer the question?
You are told that the relationship between the amount of substance formed at an electrode is directly proportional to the amount of current passed through the solution. It also states that the proportionality constant is the gram equivalent weight of the substance. You are also told that 1 Coulomb = 1 amp-s; 1 Faraday = 96500 coulombs = 1 mole of e⁻ You are also given the mw of Cl

STEP 3 = > Use the relevant data to solve the question
So once again, we must write the equation, this time for the oxidation of Cl.
$Cl^- \rightarrow Cl_2 (g) + 2e^-$; from the previous question you know that the process required 139855.07 C
So, (139855.07C) (1 mol e⁻/96500 C)(1mol Cl_2/ 2 mol e⁻) (71g Cl_2/ 1 mol Cl_2) = 51.4g

UNIT 5

Question 15 - 20

Question 15

STEP 1 = > <u>What do you need to determine to solve the problem?</u>
The number of L of air a diver will have if 300 L of air is taken to 30 m

STEP 2 = > <u>What relevant data provided in this problem is necessary in order to answer the question?</u>
You are told that the volume of gas is inversely proportional to the pressure according to Boyle's law. In addition, for every 10 meters of depth, the pressure will increase by 1 atm.

STEP 3 = > <u>Use the relevant data to solve the question</u>
So, you know that $P_1/V_1 = P_2/V_2$ according to Boyle's law as stated in the passage. You are told that at sea level, you have 300 L of air, and that will be taken to 30 meters. Since the pressure increases by 1 atm for every 10 meters of depth, you know that from sea level to 10 meters the pressure increases from 1 atm to 2 atm. So at 30 meters, the pressure will be 4 atm
So 1 atm/300 L = 4 atm/ V_2
V_2 = 300/ 4 = 75 L – the answer is B.

Question 16

STEP 1 = > <u>What do you need to determine to solve the problem?</u>
The partial pressures of oxygen and nitrogen at 22 meters

STEP 2 = > <u>What relevant data provided in this problem is necessary in order to answer the question?</u>
You are told that for every 10 meters of depth, the pressure will increase by 1 atm. In addition, you are told that the partial pressure of a gas is equal to the amount of that gas in the mixture multiplied by the pressure. You are also told that compressed air consists of 21% oxygen and 79% nitrogen

STEP 3 = > <u>Use the relevant data to solve the question</u>
The pressure at 22 meters will be 3.2 atm
So, the partial pressure of oxygen = 3.2 x 0.21 = 0.67
The partial pressure of nitrogen = 3.2 x 0.79 = 2.53
The answer is A.

Question 17

STEP 1 = > What do you need to determine to solve the problem?
The depth at which a diver can start experiencing nitrogen narcosis

STEP 2 = > What relevant data provided in this problem is necessary in order to answer the question?
You are told that for every 10 meters of depth, the pressure will increase by 1 atm. In addition, you are told that the partial pressure of a gas is equal to the amount of that gas in the mixture multiplied by the pressure. You are also told that compressed air consists of 21% oxygen and 79% nitrogen. Nitrogen narcosis can be experienced at partial pressures of 2.2 atm.

STEP 3 = > Use the relevant data to solve the question
So, you need to determine the pressure that results in a 2.2 atm partial pressure of nitrogen
2.2 atm = 0.79 x P
P = 2.8 atm
Since the pressure increases by 1 atm for every 10 m, the depth that would produce this pressure would be 18 m. The answer is C.

Question 18

STEP 1 = > What do you need to determine to solve the problem?
How the armored suits prevent DCS

STEP 2 = > What relevant data provided in this problem is necessary in order to answer the question?

You are told that DCS occurs because the partial pressure acting on the blood or tissue increases with increasing pressure, and then decreases too quickly to continue to hold the gas in solution if the ascent is too fast, so it rapidly comes out of solution.

STEP 3 = > Use the relevant data to solve the question
Since pressure increases with descent, the partial pressure of nitrogen will increase. The armoured suits are able to withstand the change in pressure with depth because they are inflexible. So the answer is B since the air being breathed by the diver is at the same pressure as air on the surface.

Question 19

STEP 1 = > What do you need to determine to solve the problem?
The maximum depth a diver can dive while breathing compressed air before they may start to encounter oxygen toxicity

STEP 2 = > What relevant data provided in this problem is necessary in order to answer the question?
Oxygen toxicity starts to become a problem when oxygen is breathed at partial pressures above 1.4 atm. In addition, you are told that the partial pressure of a gas is equal to the amount of that gas in the mixture multiplied by the pressure, and that compressed air consists of 21% oxygen and 79% nitrogen

STEP 3 = > Use the relevant data to solve the question
So, you need to determine at what pressure you will achieve a PPo_2 of 1.4 atm
1.4 atm = 0.21 x P
P = 6.7 atm
Since pressure increases by 1 atm with every 10 meters, the depth = 6.7 x 10m – 1 atm
Depth = 57 m
Answer D.

Question 20

STEP 1 = > What do you need to determine to solve the problem?
Which statements are true regarding the use of a trimix mixture with 10% oxygen, 50% helium, and 40% nitrogen

STEP 2 = > What relevant data provided in this problem is necessary in order to answer the question?
For this question, you must look back to all of the previous questions and the passage. You are told that oxygen toxicity can become a problem with increased partial pressure of oxygen, that nitrogen narcosis can become a problem with increased partial pressure of nitrogen, DCS can become a problem with increased partial pressure of a gas over a liquid followed by a rapid decrease in the partial pressure of that gas.

STEP 3 = > Use the relevant data to solve the question
Examine the 4 statements. The first is the ability to dive deeper. Statement (i) is true because the decreases in the percentages of oxygen and nitrogen in the gas mixture will decrease their partial pressures at depth, so there will be a decreased chance of oxygen toxicity and nitrogen narcosis. This means that statement (iii) is correct as well. Statement (ii) is incorrect because due to the presence of nitrogen in the mixture and helium in the mixture, both gases can absorb into the tissues and come out too quickly if the ascent is too quick. Statement (iv) is incorrect, there is no information provided that would indicate this possibility, and air consumption will be dependant on depth and personal breathing capacities. The correct answer is C.

UNIT 6

Questions 21–22

Question 21

STEP 1 = > <u>What do you need to determine to solve the problem?</u>
Which equation represents the Van der Waals equation

STEP 2 = > <u>What relevant data provided in this problem is necessary in order to</u>
<u>answer the question?</u>
You are given two equations to account for the deviations from the ideal gas equation
due to size and stickiness. In addition, you are provided with the ideal gas equation

STEP 3 = > <u>Use the relevant data to solve the question</u>
Given that $PV = nRT$
And $P_{ideal} = P_{real} + a\,(n^2/V^2)$
And $V_{ideal} = V_{real} - nb$
So use the ideal gas equation and plug in the new expressions for P and V
$[P + a\,(n^2/V^2)][V - nB] = nRT$

Now, solve for P
$[P + a\,(n^2/V^2)] = nRT/(V-nb)$
$P = nRT/(V-nb) - an^2/V^2$; the answer is D

Question 22

STEP 1 = > <u>What do you need to determine to solve the problem?</u>
How many moles of gas are in the sample indicated in the graph

STEP 2 = > <u>What relevant data provided in this problem is necessary in order to</u>
<u>answer the question?</u>
You are given a graph of P vs. $1/V$, and told that 1 atm = 760 and the value of the gas
constant R. In addition, the questions state that the slope of the graph is equal to PV.
The passage gives you the ideal gas equation $PV = nRT$

STEP 3 = > <u>Use the relevant data to solve the question</u>
So, $PV = nRT$
Since the slope of the graph = rise/run – simply pick two sets of points on the graph to
find the slope. So, slope = $(900-200)/(0.045-0.01) = 700/0.035 = 20000$
So PV = 20000 torr-L, this must be converted to atm-L so, divide by 760
$PV = 26.32$
Since $PV = nRT$
26.32 atm-L = n (0.08206 atm-L/mol-K)(273K)
n = 1.17 mol; answer B.

UNIT 7

Questions 23–27

Question 23

STEP 1 = > What do you need to determine to solve the problem?
The question requires you to identify the point at which all three phases of matter coexist.
To do so, you must understand how to read the phase diagram.

STEP 2 = > What relevant data provided in this problem is necessary in order to answer the question?
The passage indicates that each region represents a phase and each line is a phase boundary, where two phases coexist.
Therefore the triple point, where all three phases are present, must be at the intersection of all three regions and lines.

STEP 3 = > Use the relevant data to solve the question
Choice A is a point in the gas phase, Choice B is a point in the gas phase near the gas-liquid phase boundary, and Choice C is a point in the solid region of the diagram.
However, Choice D is located at the intersection of all three regions and boundaries and is therefore the triple point.

Question 24

STEP 1 = > What do you need to determine to solve the problem?
The question requires you to identify the phase of the material in the diagram at room temperature and atmospheric pressure.
To do so, you must locate those conditions on the diagram.

STEP 2 = > What relevant data provided in this problem is necessary in order to answer the question?
The passage indicates which region of the diagram corresponds to each phase, allowing you to determine the phase under standard conditions from its location on the diagram.

STEP 3 = > Use the relevant data to solve the question
Room temperature is approximately 25° and atmospheric pressure is 1 atm, which places the point in the bottom region of the diagram, which corresponds to the gas phase.

Question 25

STEP 1 = > What do you need to determine to solve the problem?
The question requires you to identify the phase change that accompanies the given change of conditions. To do so, you must determine what phase boundary is crossed.

STEP 2 = > What relevant data provided in this problem is necessary in order to answer the question?
The passage indicates which region corresponds to each phase, and that crossing a phase boundary leads to a direct change from one phase to another.

STEP 3 = > Use the relevant data to solve the question
The starting point can be located in the solid region, and the decrease in pressure crosses into the gas region.
Therefore, the change is from solid directly to gas. Deposition is the change from gas to solid, evaporation is from liquid to gas, and fusion is from gas to liquid. Sublimation is the process by which a solid changes directly to a gas.

Question 26

STEP 1 = > What do you need to determine to solve the problem?
The question requires you to make a determination about the relative densities of the solid and liquid phases. To do so, you must understand what the passage can indicate about phase density.

STEP 2 = > What relevant data provided in this problem is necessary in order to answer the question?
The passage indicates that going up on the diagram represents an increase in pressure, and that the lines represent phase boundaries.

STEP 3 = > Use the relevant data to solve the question
Since an increase in pressure causes materials to attempt to decrease in volume, increasing pressure and seeing what phase transitions occur can tell you about the densities of the phases.
The slope of the liquid-solid phase boundary indicates that at constant temperature, an increase in pressure will eventually lead to solidification. This indicates that the volume of an equal mass of material must be lower in the solid phase, and the solid phase is therefore denser than the liquid phase.

Question 27

STEP 1 = > What do you need to determine to solve the problem?
The question requires you to identify the vapor pressure of the material at a given temperature.
To do so, you must locate the phase boundary at that temperature.

STEP 2 = > What relevant data provided in this problem is necessary in order to answer the question?
The passage indicates that the phase boundaries represent the conditions at which phase changes occur.

STEP 3 = > Use the relevant data to solve the question
The vapor pressure at a certain temperature is the pressure at which the gas-liquid phase transition occurs, so it must be on the gas-liquid phase boundary line.
At 150°, the phase boundary is located at approximately 6 atm.

UNIT 8

Questions 28–32

Question 28

STEP 1 = > What do you need to determine to solve the problem?
The question requires you to identify the best acid for preparing a particular buffer.
To do so, you must understand what makes a buffer effective.

STEP 2 = > What relevant data provided in this problem is necessary in order to answer the question?
The passage indicates that buffers can perform best at pH close to their acid pKa, which gives them the most flexibility and buffer capacity.

STEP 3 = > Use the relevant data to solve the question
The desired buffer pH is 8.0, and the acid which has the closest pKa to that is hypochlorous acid, which has a pKa of 7.50.
Therefore the best solution for the desired buffer would be hypochlorous acid and hypochlorite.

Question 29

STEP 1 = > What do you need to determine to solve the problem?
The question require you to determine the approximate base:acid concentration ratio in human blood.
To do so, you must calculate how the concentration ratio changes buffer pH.

STEP 2 = > What relevant data provided in this problem is necessary in order to answer the question?
The passage indicates that the Henderson-Hasselbach equation governs buffer pH, and that pH is simply the pKa of the acid modified by the log of the base:acid concentration ratio.

STEP 3 = > Use the relevant data to solve the question
Since the blood pH is 7.4 and the pKa of carbonic acid is 6.37, the concentration modifier is almost exactly 1.
Therefore, the log of the concentration ratio must be 1. The antilog of 1 is 10, meaning that the ratio of bicarbonate to carbonic acid in the blood is about 10:1.

Question 30

STEP 1 = > What do you need to determine to solve the problem?
The question requires you to calculate the pH of the given buffer solution.
To do so, you must apply the Henderson-Hasselbach equation.

STEP 2 = > What relevant data provided in this problem is necessary in order to answer the question?
The passage indicates that the pH of a buffer is equal to the pKa of its acid plus the log of the base:acid concentration ratio.

STEP 3 = > Use the relevant data to solve the question
The pKa of ammonium is 9.25.
The acid:base ratio is 5:1, which means that the base:acid ratio is 1:5. The log of 1/5 is difficult to calculate by hand, but it must be between 0 and -1, which correspond to ratios of 1:1 and 1:10. It can be roughly estimated to be between about -0.6 and -0.8. The only choice that falls into that range from 9.25 is 8.5, which is the correct answer. The actual pH of the given buffer is 8.55.

Question 31

STEP 1 = > What do you need to determine to solve the problem?
The question requires you to determine the relative capacity of the given buffer. To do so, you must identify the factors that influence buffer capacity.

STEP 2 = > What relevant data provided in this problem is necessary in order to answer the question?
The passage indicates that buffer capacity is a measure of how much acid or base can be absorbed by the buffer solution without exhausting it.
Acids are neutralized by the buffer base and bases are neutralized by the buffer acid.

STEP 3 = > Use the relevant data to solve the question
Since the buffer pH is 5 and the pKa of acetic acid is 4.76, the concentration modifier in the Henderson-Hasselbach equation is positive.
This means that there must be more base than acid in the solution. Since the acetate reacts with acids and the acetic acid reacts with bases, the buffer must be able to absorb more acid due to its higher concentration of acetate.

Question 32

STEP 1 = > What do you need to determine to solve the problem?
The question requires you to calculate the amount of base necessary to create the desired buffer.
To do so, you must determine what the effect of the base will be.

STEP 2 = > What relevant data provided in this problem is necessary in order to answer the question?
The passage indicates that the pH of a buffer is equal to the pKa of the acid when equal amounts of the buffer acid and its conjugate base are present.

STEP 3 = > Use the relevant data to solve the question
Since the pKa of phenol and the desired pH are approximately equal, the desired concentration ratio is 1:1.
Therefore, the sodium hydroxide should be used to create an equal amount of phenol and phenoxide. Each molecule of sodium hydroxide will react with one of phenol to form a single phenoxide ion. Since the 10 mmol of phenol is the only source of the buffer material, it must be divided into equal parts phenol and phenoxide, half and half. Therefore, it is necessary to react the phenol with 5 mmol of sodium hydroxide to produce 5 mmol of sodium phenoxide and leave 5 mmol of phenol, giving a buffer of pH □ 10.

Solutions: **Organic Chemistry**

UNIT 1

Questions 1–3

Question 1

STEP 1 = > <u>What do you need to determine to solve the problem?</u>
Which molecule does not fit the criteria for a glucocorticoid according to the passage

STEP 2 = > <u>What relevant data provided in this problem is necessary in order to answer the question?</u>
A general 17 carbon ring structure of adrenocortical hormones is shown.
In addition, the passage states that a glucocorticoid must possess the following:

1. It must have 21 carbons

2. There must be a methyl group attached to carbons 10 and 13

3. There must be an oxygen base bonded to carbon 11

4. Carbon 20 must be a carbonyl group

5. Carbon 21 must have an oxygen base bonded to it

STEP 3 = > <u>Use the relevant data to solve the question</u>
Now, you must examine the different structures provided and determine which ones fit these criteria and find the one that doesn't. All four molecules have 21 carbons. The molecule that does not fit the criteria is molecule A. It does not have an O-bonded to carbon 11, it has a methyl. In addition, there is an O-bonded to carbon 13 instead of another methyl group. So, the answer is A.

Question 2

STEP 1 = > <u>What do you need to determine to solve the problem?</u>
Which molecule is an estrogen

STEP 2 = > <u>What relevant data provided in this problem is necessary in order to answer the question?</u>
A general 17 carbon ring structure of adrenocortical hormones is shown.
In addition, the passage states that an estrogen must possess the following:

1. It must be an 18 carbon adrenocortical hormone

2. It must have a methyl group attached to carbon 13

STEP 3 = > Use the relevant data to solve the question
All of the molecules fit criteria 1 and 2. However, only one of the molecules has a benzene ring. The correct answer is C.

Question 3

STEP 1 = > What do you need to determine to solve the problem?
Which statement is true regarding androstenedione

STEP 2 = > What relevant data provided in this problem is necessary in order to answer the question?
The structure of androstenedione is provided. In addition, you are told that the androgens are responsible for male secondary characteristics, and that anabolic steroids mimic the male sex hormones (thus, anabolic steroids mimic the androgens).
A general 17 carbon ring structure of adrenocortical hormones is shown.
In addition, the passage states that an androgen must possess the following:

     1. It must be an 19 carbon adrenocortical hormone
     2. It must have methyl groups attached to carbons 10 and 13
     3. It must have a benzene ring on the ring containing carbons 1-5

STEP 3 = > Use the relevant data to solve the question
The statements involving oxygen are obviously untrue since the passage states nothing about the requirement of oxygen in the structure of the androgens. The answer is D. As stated above, androstenedione contains methyl groups attached to carbons 10 and 13 which is a requirement in the androgen structure. Thus, this molecule can mimic an androgen and is therefore an anabolic steroid.

UNIT 2

Question 4

Question 4

STEP 1 = > What do you need to determine to solve the problem?
Which molecule is the toxin of the Christmas rose

STEP 2 = > What relevant data provided in this problem is necessary in order to answer the question?
You are told that cardiac glycosides have a steroid component and a sugar component. The structure of the steroid portion is similar to the general structure of the adrenocorticoids, except a butaryolactone ring or pyrone ring will be attached to carbon 17. A methyl group must be attached to carbon 13. The glycoside must be attached to an O-bonded to carbon 3. You are given the structure of butaryolactone and pyrone rings. The general 17 carbon ring structure of adrenocortical hormones is shown in the initial passage.

STEP 3 = > Use the relevant data to solve the question
Again, you must simply examine the molecules to find the one that fits the criteria given above. The correct answer is A. This molecule has a pyrone ring attached to carbon 17. In addition, there is a sugar bonded to an O-bonded to carbon 3. Finally, there is a methyl group bonded to carbon 13.

UNIT 3

Questions 5-8

Question 5

STEP 1 = > What do you need to determine to solve the problem?
What are n, m and p for oleic acid

STEP 2 = > What relevant data provided in this problem is necessary in order to answer the question?
You are given a table with the chemical formulas of a variety of different fatty acids. In addition, you are told that saturated fatty acids have no double bonds, while unsaturated fatty acids haves have one or more double bonds. You are given the following general formula:

$$CH_3(CH_2)_n(CH=CHCH_2)_m(CH_2)_pCOOH$$

STEP 3 = > Use the relevant data to solve the question

The chemical formula of oleic acid given in the table is $C_{18}H_{34}O_2$. One carbon and one hydrogen belong to the carboxylic acid group (COOH), so that leaves 17 carbons and 33 hydrogens for the rest of the molecule. If the 17 carbons were fully saturated, the end carbon would have 3 H's, and the other 16 carbons would have 2H's each, for a total of 35 H's. However, there are only 33 H's, which means that two H's are absent so there must be an unsaturated part of the chain. For every two H's removed from a completely saturated fatty acid chain, there will be one double bond. So, m must equal 1. D is the only option where m = 1, in addition, when the other numbers are plugged into the formula, this gives 13 CH_2 groups for a total of 13 carbons and 26 H's. Add to this the 3 C's and 4 H's from the m group and the 1 C and 3 H's from the end methyl group and you have 17 C's and 33 H's. Add the COOH group and you get 18 C's, 34 H's, and 2 O's. The correct answer is D.

Question 6

STEP 1 = > What do you need to determine to solve the problem?
Which represents arachidonic acid

STEP 2 = > What relevant data provided in this problem is necessary in order to answer the question?
You are given a table with the chemical formulas of a variety of different fatty acids. In addition, you are told that saturated fatty acids have no double bonds, while unsaturated fatty acids haves have one or more double bonds. You are given the following general formula:
$CH_3(CH_2)_n(CH=CHCH_2)_m(CH_2)_pCOOH$
In addition, you are told that omega fatty acids only have cis unsaturated bonds

STEP 3 = > Use the relevant data to solve the question
Since arachidonic acid is an omega fatty acid, you can immediately discard answers B and D, as these both show trans bonds and are therefore incorrect. Now, you must go to the table and get the formula for arachidonic acid, which is $C_{20}H_{32}O_2$. Taking away the C and H for the COOH group gives 19 C's and 31 H's. If the chain was fully saturated there would need to be 3 H's for the end C and 2 for every other carbon (36 H's) for a total of 39, however there are only 31 hydrogens available for the chain (don't forget to subtract one H for the COOH group), so 8 are missing. This means there must be 4 double bonds. So, looking at the structures, both A and C have 20 C's, but the correct answer is C because it has 4 double bonds in the cis configuration.

Question 7

STEP 1 = > What do you need to determine to solve the problem?
What type of omega fatty acid is oleic acid

STEP 2 = > What relevant data provided in this problem is necessary in order to answer the question?
You are given a table with the chemical formulas of a variety of different fatty acids. In addition, you are told that saturated fatty acids have no double bonds, while unsaturated fatty acids haves have one or more double bonds. You are given the following general formula:
$CH_3(CH_2)_n(CH=CHCH_2)_m(CH_2)_pCOOH$
In addition, you are told that omega fatty acids only have cis unsaturated bonds. You are also told that the classification of an omega fatty acid can be obtained by subtracting the highest double-bond locant in the scientific name from the number of carbons in the fatty acid, and was shown an example with linolenic acid.

STEP 3 = > Use the relevant data to solve the question
First, you need to determine the structure of oleic acid. You are given that n = 7. So, taking
the formula from the table: $C_{18}H_{34}O_2$, you must determine m and p first. Taking away the
COOH group at the end leaves 17 C's and 33 H's. Taking away the end methyl group leaves
16 C's and 30 H's. If the chain was fully saturated 32 H's would be necessary, but 2 are
missing so there must be 1 double bond. This means that m = 1 and p = 6. So, the structure
of oleic acid must be as follows:

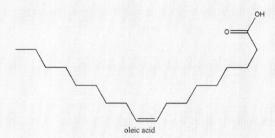

oleic acid

Starting with the carbonyl carbon as #1, the double bond is at carbon # 9. Since this is an
18 carbon chain, simply subtract 18 – 9 = 9. So, oleic acid is an omega 9 fatty acid, and
hence the answer is C.

Question 8

STEP 1 = > What do you need to determine to solve the problem?
The correct order for the melting temperatures.

STEP 2 = > What relevant data provided in this problem is necessary in order to answer the question?
You are given a table with the chemical formulas of a variety of different fatty acids. In addition, you are told that saturated fatty acids have no double bonds, while unsaturated fatty acids haves have one or more double bonds. You are given the following general formula:

$$CH_3(CH_2)_n(CH=CHCH_2)_m(CH_2)_pCOOH$$

In addition, you are told that increases in intermolecular interactions between the hydrocarbon chains of fatty acids results in an increase in the melting point of the fatty acids

STEP 3 = > Use the relevant data to solve the question
Increases in intermolecular interactions would occur with increasing chain length because there would be more area to interact. In addition, an increase in the number of unsaturated bonds would disrupt the ability of the chains to interact due to the limited mobility at a double bond, so this would cause a decrease in melting temperature. So, first take the formulas of each of the fatty acids in question from the chart.

  (i)   Docosahexaenoic acid $C_{22}H_{32}O_2$
  (ii)   Arachidic acid $C_{20}H_{40}O_2$
  (iii)   Behenic acid $C_{22}H_{44}O_2$
  (iv)   Arachidonic acid $C_{20}H_{32}O_2$

Determine the amount of unsaturation in each fatty acid. For (i), a 22 carbon chain would need 44 H's to be completely saturated. Since 12 H's are missing for (i), there must be 6 double bonds in that molecule. For (ii), a 20 carbon chain would need 40 H's to be completely saturated so there are no double bonds in that molecule. For (iii), there are no double bonds, and (iv) has four double bonds. So, since (iv) has only a 20 C chain and four double bonds, its melting temp should be the lowest. Because molecule (i) has 6 double bonds, it will not be able to pack as tightly as (ii) even though it has more carbons, so it will have the next lowest. Molecule (iii) will have the highest melting point because it has a longer chain than ii and has no unsaturated bonds. So, the order from lowest to highest is (iv) < (i) < (ii) < (iii), answer is B.
Thus, this molecule fits the criteria for a cardiac glycoside.

UNIT 4

Questions 9-12

Question 9

STEP 1 => What do you need to determine to solve the problem?
The structure of anandamide.

STEP 2 => What relevant data provided in this problem is necessary in order to answer the question?
You are told that anandamide is a member of a certain family of compounds that can be made in the lab by combining a fatty acid with an ethanolamine. In addition, a general reaction scheme which starts with a fatty acid, is activated with n-hydroxysuccinimide. It then reacted with ethanolamine to give a molecule with the fatty acid chain minus the OH group attached to the amine group (NH_2) of the ethanolamine. Finally, the question states that anandamide can be made from arachidonic acid, and the structure of arachidonic acid is provided.

STEP 3 => Use the relevant data to solve the question
The important issue for this question is to ignore all of the intermediate steps and simply look at the starting fatty acid structure and how it is changed in the ending product when the ethanolamine is added to it. In this case, you see that the ethanolamine retains its entire structure and the fatty acid loses the OH at the end of the chain and the carbon then forms a bond with the amine group of the ethanolamine. Answer D can be immediately discarded because it does not contain any nitrogen. Now, to determine the correct answer, simply count the number of carbons in the chain and note the positions of the double bonds. The correct answer is C.

Question 10

STEP 1 => What do you need to determine to solve the problem?
The structure of the side product formed during the given reaction

STEP 2 => What relevant data provided in this problem is necessary in order to answer the question?
The structure of dicyclohexylcarbodiimde (DCC) is given, and it is explained that the side product forms by the reaction of DCC and water. You know the structure of water is H_2O.

STEP 3 => Use the relevant data to solve the question
Recall that hydrolysis at a double bond will result in the breaking of that double bond. In this case, DCC has two N-C double bonds in the centre of the molecule. O is highly electronegative so will be attracted to the double bonds and result in the formation of a new double-bonded O attached to the original DCC molecule. Therefore, the answer is A.

Question 11

STEP 1 => What do you need to determine to solve the problem?
Which molecules of those listed can be attached to a fatty acid to produce a surfactant

STEP 2 => What relevant data provided in this problem is necessary in order to answer the question?
The question states that a surfactant contains both a hydrophilic and hydrophobic component. Recall that hydrophilic means "water loving" and hydrophobic means "water hating." Long hydrocarbon chains such as fatty acid chains are highly hydrophobic. So, the hydrophilic molecules need to be determined

STEP 3 => Use the relevant data to solve the question
The molecules displayed in I and II have an abundance of O and N within the molecules. The larger the content of OH and NH groups, the more hydrophilic the molecules become. Molecule III contains no OH or NH groups and has two benzene rings which are highly hydrophobic. Therefore, the answer is D.

Question 12

STEP 1 => What do you need to determine to solve the problem?
What molecule would need to be reacted with activated oleic acid to produce oleamide

STEP 2 => What relevant data provided in this problem is necessary in order to answer the question?
You are told that oleamide can be produced by a similar reaction as the fatty acid ethanolamides, so again you are dealing with the original set of reactions given. Again, try to ignore the irrelevant details in the reaction and simply look at the final resulting molecule. You can see that the ethanolamide is simply attached to the carbonyl carbon of the initial fatty acid chain with a loss of the terminal OH group from the fatty acid chain.

STEP 3 => Use the relevant data to solve the question
Now, examine the structure of oleamide. Note that the only changes to the oleic acid are the loss of an OH and an addition of an NH_2. Thus, the answer is A.

UNIT 5

Questions 13–16

Question 13

STEP 1 => What do you need to determine to solve the problem?
What molecule could you react with butane-2,3-diamine to produce 2,3,5,6 tetramethyl pyrazine

STEP 2 => What relevant data provided in this problem is necessary in order to answer the question?
The question provides a reaction with 2,3-diamine to produce the heterocycle 2,3,5,6 tetramethyl pyrazine. In addition it states that this type of reaction can take place with nitrogen nucleophiles and carbonyl or halide compounds.

STEP 3 => Use the relevant data to solve the question
In the case of the example reaction, the reaction is occurring with a carbonyl compound. Since it states that this reaction can occur with halide compounds, find the answer that is a similar structure to the carbonyl compound in the example reaction, but where the carbonyls have been replaced with a halide. Thus, the answer is B.

Question 14

STEP 1 => What do you need to determine to solve the problem?
What would be the product formed when butane-2,3-diamine was reacted with

STEP 2 => What relevant data provided in this problem is necessary in order to answer the question?
The question provides a reaction with 2,3-diamine to produce the heterocycle 2,3,5,6 tetramethyl pyrazine. In addition it states that this type of reaction can take place with nitrogen nucleophiles and carbonyl or halide compounds. In the reaction given, it shows that the two molecules will combine through the loss of the oxygen groups in the form of water. The oxygen groups are lost and a new bond is formed where O used to be and N from the other molecule. In addition, the double bond on the O shifts to a double bond between the two carbons of the original molecule.

STEP 3 => Use the relevant data to solve the question
In the case of halide compounds, the halide will be lost in the form of HX (where X is any halide). A new bond will form between the N and where the halide was formerly attached. For this molecule, there is both an O and a Cl group, so both will be lost and new bonds will form with the N groups on the 2,3-diamine. Therefore, the resulting product will be the original 2,3-diamine with two new bonds that form a 5-membered ring. The answer is A.

Question 15

STEP 1 => What do you need to determine to solve the problem?
Which molecule is lost during the heterocycle reaction

STEP 2 => What relevant data provided in this problem is necessary in order to answer the question?
The question says that the reaction is a substitution or condensation reaction. In the example reaction, it is stated that the reaction occurs with the loss of a water molecule from the original reactants. This means that both H's and O's must be removed from the reactants. The H comes from the diamine, and the O from the carbonyl groups of the other molecule.

STEP 3 => Use the relevant data to solve the question
In this case, there is both a Cl and an O group that will be removed from the reactant prior to heterocyclization. When combined with the H's from the diamine, this means that both water and HCl will be formed and lost from the resulting product. Therefore, the answer is B.

Question 16

STEP 1 => What do you need to determine to solve the problem?
Which one of the choices will be the product P of the given reaction

STEP 2 => What relevant data provided in this problem is necessary in order to answer the question?
Again, you have the example reaction to follow, and you are provided with a molecule containing both carbonyl and Cl groups that will be involved in the reaction. The molecule is being reacted simply with amine.

STEP 3 => Use the relevant data to solve the question
In the reaction with amine, H's will be lost from the amine, and the O and Cl will be lost from the other molecule. The new product will simply involve two new bonds between the carbons formerly containing Cl and O and the N of the amine. This will result in a 7-membered ring. So the answer is C.

UNIT 6

Questions 17–20

Question 17

STEP 1 => What do you need to determine to solve the problem?
Which molecule is necessary to form ethene from bromoethane

STEP 2 => What relevant data provided in this problem is necessary in order to answer the question?
The problems states that an alkene is formed by the elimination reaction of an alcohol in a strong acid or a halide in a strong base.

STEP 3 => Use the relevant data to solve the question

Since bromoehane is a halide, a strong base is necessary to remove the Br and form an alkene. A is a strong acid, B is neither, and C is a strong base. The answer is C.

Question 18

STEP 1 => What do you need to determine to solve the problem?

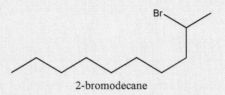

2-bromodecane

Starting with 2-bromodecane , what alkene could be formed by an elimination reaction

STEP 2 => What relevant data provided in this problem is necessary in order to answer the question?
The problem states that an alkene is formed by the elimination reaction of an alcohol in a strong acid or a halide in a strong base. Alkenes are molecules with at least 1 double carbon bond in them. You need to recall that decane is 10 carbons, so 2-bromo decane would be a 10 carbon chain with a Br group at the second position.

STEP 3 => Use the relevant data to solve the question
Because of the location of the Br group, the removal of the Br group could result in a double-bond forming either between C1 and C2 or C2 and C3. In this case, the only possible answer among those given is D where the double bond is between C2 and C3.

Question 19

STEP 1 => What do you need to determine to solve the problem?
Which molecule is formed by an addition reaction with HCl

STEP 2 => What relevant data provided in this problem is necessary in order to answer the question?
The problem states that an alkene is formed by the elimination reaction of an alcohol in a strong acid or a halide in a strong base. Alkenes are molecules with at least 1-double bond carbon in them. It also says that an addition reaction is the opposite of an elimination reaction, so you know that a double-bond carbon will be broken and that groups will be added at that position on the original molecule.

STEP 3 => Use the relevant data to solve the question
In this case, HCl is being added to the alkene. This means that there is an H and a Cl that can be added where the double bond in the molecule exists. Therefore, the answer will be B.

Question 20

STEP 1 => What do you need to determine to solve the problem?
Why one predominates over the other when two different possibilities exist in the
product of an addition reaction with an alkene

STEP 2 => What relevant data provided in this problem is necessary in order to answer
the question?
It is stated that an addition reaction is the opposite of an elimination, which means that
a double bond will be broken and two groups will be added to the original alkene. In
addition, Markovnikov's rule states that in additions of HX to unsymmetrical alkenes,
the H^+ of HX goes to the double-bonded carbon that already has the greatest number
of hydrogens.

STEP 3 => Use the relevant data to solve the question
For this problem, steric hindrance has absolutely nothing to do with the reaction
occurring. In this case, the bond is breaking and groups are being added, one of them
being an H. When the H is added, a carbo cation will be formed on the other carbon
that was formerly involved in the double bond. The most stable form of this carbo
cation will determine which molecule predominates, so the answer is B.

UNIT 7

Questions 21–24

Question 21

STEP 1 => What do you need to determine to solve the problem?
Which molecule contains a hemiacetal group

STEP 2 => What relevant data provided in this problem is necessary in order to answer the
question?
The question provides the general structure of a hemiacetal. Hemiacetals contain an OH
and an OR group which are bonded to the same carbon.

STEP 3 => Use the relevant data to solve the question
The only molecule listed that has both an OH and an OR bonded to the same carbon is I.
Therefore, the answer is A.

Question 22

STEP 1 => What do you need to determine to solve the problem?
Which molecules are formed when the given molecule forms a hemiacetal ring

STEP 2 => What relevant data provided in this problem is necessary in order to answer the question?
The question states that when a molecule has an OH group γ or δ to an aldehyde or ketone carbonyl group, the molecule undergoes an intra-molecular reaction to form a five or six-membered hemiacetal ring. In addition, an example cyclization is shown. In this case, the double-bonded O breaks one of the bonds and the electrons go to the O so that a new OH can frm. The O-bonded to either the γ or δ carbon will then bond with the carbonyl carbon to form a 5 or 6-membered ring

STEP 3 => Use the relevant data to solve the question
In this case, there is both a group γ or δ to an aldehyde or ketone carbonyl group so two rings will form a 5-membered ring and a 6-membered ring. Push the electrons and bonds around as described above. The new bond to form the ring will form between the O attached to either the γ or δ carbon and the carbonyl carbon. Therefore, the answer is B.

Question 23

STEP 1 => What do you need to determine to solve the problem?
The most stable form of the molecule drawn

STEP 2 => What relevant data provided in this problem is necessary in order to answer the question?
The question states that when a molecule has an OH group γ or δ to an aldehyde or ketone carbonyl group, the molecule undergoes an intra-molecular reaction to form a five or six-membered hemiacetal ring. In addition, it says that unless the hemiacetal forms a ring, it is more stable in the aldehyde form

STEP 3 => Use the relevant data to solve the question
By examining the original molecule, two things are apparent. First, the molecule contains Oh groups γ or δ to an aldehyde or ketone, so a cyclization will take place. In addition, there is an extra singly bonded OR group that would be more stable in the aldehyde or ketone form, so a double bond will form with the O. Once the molecule has formed a ring and a C=O, the result will be D.

Question 24

STEP 1 => What do you need to determine to solve the problem?
Which molecule drawn will form the most stable hydrate

STEP 2 => What relevant data provided in this problem is necessary in order to answer the question?
The question provides a general structure for a hydrate and says that a hydrate can be formed from an aldehyde or ketone

STEP 3 => Use the relevant data to solve the question
The three molecules shown are all either an aldehyde or a ketone, so they can all form hydrates. Stability is influenced greatly by the types of chemical groups surrounding the site of interest (in this case, the carbonyl bond C=O). Of the three molecules, only the first one contains Cl groups, which are highly electronegative. Due to the equal electron withdrawing properties of the Cl's, this molecule will form the most stable hydrate so the answer is A.

UNIT 8

Questions 25–27

Question 25

STEP 1 => What do you need to determine to solve the problem?
What is the new amino acid formed via the transamination process

STEP 2 => What relevant data provided in this problem is necessary in order to answer the question?
A general reaction is given which shows a keto acid reacting with an amino acid to form a new amino acid. In this reaction, the R and R' groups on the amino acid and the keto acid are simply exchanged

STEP 3 => Use the relevant data to solve the question
If you simply swap the side groups between the keto acid and the amino acid give, you will get answer A as the new amino acid is formed.

Question 26

STEP 1 => What do you need to determine to solve the problem?
Which molecules could represent possible intermediates in the transamination process

STEP 2 => What relevant data provided in this problem is necessary in order to answer the question?
The passage says that the transamination process occurs via imine intermediates. It also explains that imines are a double-bonded carbon to an N (C=N).

STEP 3 => Use the relevant data to solve the question
Simply examine the possible structures and find the ones that contain C=N bonds. In this case, only molecules I and III have this in their structure so the answer is D.

Question 27

STEP 1 => What do you need to determine to solve the problem?
What molecule would be necessary to transform serine to threonine via a transamination process

STEP 2 => What relevant data provided in this problem is necessary in order to answer the question?
The question provides the general reaction of how to convert one amino acid to another via the transamination process. The keto acid and the old amino acid simply swap side groups (R and R') to form a new keto acid and a new amino acid.

STEP 3 => Use the relevant data to solve the question
To change from serine to threonine, it would be necessary to react the serine with a keto

acid containing the ⟨OH side group⟩ side group. The correct answer is D since it is the only keto acid with this side group attached shown among the answers

UNIT 9

Questions 28–31

Question 28

STEP 1 => What do you need to determine to solve the problem?
Which set of bases are demonstrating correct hydrogen bonding

STEP 2 => What relevant data provided in this problem is necessary in order to answer the question?
The passage provides an explanation of tautomers and shows the general structure of the keto and enol for of a set of tautomers. In addition, it says that the bases must take the keto form in order for hydrogen bonding to occur.

STEP 3 => Use the relevant data to solve the question
The correct answer is A, because both bases are in the keto form. In answer B, they are in the enol form, and in C and D one of the two is in the enol form.

Question 29

STEP 1 => What do you need to determine to solve the problem?
Which molecule represents the intermediate form that occurs during the transformation from glucose-6-phosphate and fructose-6-phosphate

STEP 2 => What relevant data provided in this problem is necessary in order to answer the question?
The question provides you with the structures of both the glucose and the fructose molecules. In addition, the original passage shows the general form of a tautomerism from a keto to an enol form.

STEP 3 => Use the relevant data to solve the question
Tautomerism occurs by the transformation of a keto to an enol or visa versa. Glucose-6-phosphate is in the keto form, so is fructose-6-phosphate. Therefore, the intermediate transformation must be to an enol form that is the same for both molecules. The correct answer is C.

Question 30

STEP 1 => What do you need to determine to solve the problem?
Which hydrogen indicated by the arrows is acidic in nature

STEP 2 => What relevant data provided in this problem is necessary in order to answer the question?
Examine the molecules and determine which hydrogens are alpha to the carbonyl group.

STEP 3 => Use the relevant data to solve the question
The passage states that the hydrogen alpha to a carbonyl group is acidic, this only occurs in molecule II since the H is bonded to the carbonyl carbon and therefore alpha to it. Therefore the answer is B.

Question 31

STEP 1 => What do you need to determine to solve the problem?
Which enolate would be present in the greater amount

STEP 2 => What relevant data provided in this problem is necessary in order to answer the question?
The passage provides chemical structures of the two enolates. In addition, it is explained that an enolate is simply an anion of the enol formed by the loss of an H from the carbon alpha to the carbonyl carbon.

STEP 3 => Use the relevant data to solve the question
Since both molecules have lost an H from a carbon alpha to a carbonyl carbon, they are both enolates. In this case, the two O surrounding the negative charge in compound A would help to stabilize it more, so it would be present in a greater amount than compound B. Therefore, the answer is A.

UNIT 10

Questions 32–36

Question 32

STEP 1 = > What do you need to determine to solve the problem?
How many stereo centers are in the molecule shown

STEP 2 = > What relevant data provided in this problem is necessary in order to answer the question?
You are told that a stereocenter is a carbon with 4 different attached groups.
You are also given the structure of the molecule in question

STEP 3 = > Use the relevant data to solve the question

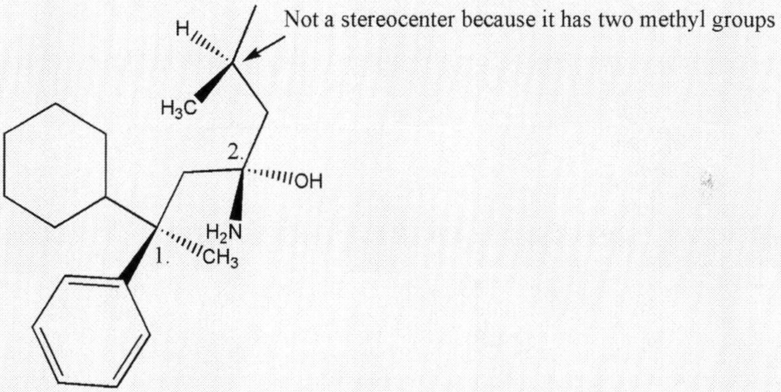

Examining the molecule we see that there are only 2 carbons that have different groups attached, so the answer is C.

Question 33

STEP 1 = > What do you need to determine to solve the problem?
Which molecule pair is diastereomers

STEP 2 = > What relevant data provided in this problem is necessary in order to answer
the question?

You are told that two molecules with the same chemical structure, but different directions
of rotation are known as diastereomers. The passage explains how stereocenters are
prioritized and then how to determine the direction of rotation thereby determining R or S
configuration. You are also told in the passage that in order for a molecule to be a stereomer,
it must have at least one stereocenter carbon – one with 4 different groups attached.

STEP 3 = > Use the relevant data to solve the question
Examine the choices closely. The molecules in choice A are exactly the same (simply
flipped vertically), and therefore cannot be diastereomers. Choices C and D do not have
any stereocenters. Therefore, by deduction, choice B is the correct answer. If you examine
the two molecules, you will see that one is R and one is S as shown.

Question 34

STEP 1 = > What do you need to determine to solve the problem?
How many diastereomers are there of threonine

STEP 2 = > What relevant data provided in this problem is necessary in order to answer
the question?
You are told that two molecules with the same chemical structure, but different directions
of rotation are known as diastereomers. The passage explains how stereocenters are
prioritized and then how to determine the direction of rotation thereby determining R or S
configuration. You are also told in the passage that in order for a molecule to be a stereomer,
it must have at least one stereocenter carbon – one with 4 different groups attached.

STEP 3 = > Use the relevant data to solve the question
First, examine the molecule to determine the number of stereocenters.

As shown, the molecule has two stereo centers. You know from the paragraph that each
of these centers can be in either the R or S configuration. So, you have the following
possibilities: R,R; S,S; R,S; S,R. The answer is D – 4.
So there are 2^n possible configurations where n is the number of stereocenters.

Question 35

STEP 1 = > What do you need to determine to solve the problem?
You need to determine the R,S configuration of the given molecule

STEP 2 = > What relevant data provided in this problem is necessary in order to answer the question?
You are told that two molecules with the same chemical structure, but different directions of rotation are known as diastereomers. The passage explains how stereocenters are prioritized and then how to determine the direction of rotation thereby determining R or S configuration. You are also told in the passage that in order for a molecule to be a stereomer, it must have at least one stereocenter carbon – one with 4 different groups attached.

STEP 3 = > Use the relevant data to solve the question
Again, examine the molecule for stereocenters, then prioritize the attached groups, then using this prioritization, determine the direction of rotation.

There are two stereocenters.

This is the R configuration

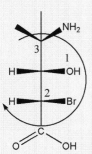

This is also the R configuration

So, the answer is A.

Note: the reason they are 2 and 4 instead of 1 and 2 is that the first carbon will be the carbonyl carbon.

Question 36

STEP 1 = > What do you need to determine to solve the problem?
You need to determine which molecule corresponds to the 2S, 3R, 4R configuration

STEP 2 = > What relevant data provided in this problem is necessary in order to answer the question?
You are told that two molecules with the same chemical structure, but different directions of rotation are known as diastereomers. The passage explains how stereocenters are prioritized and then how to determine the direction of rotation thereby determining R or S configuration. You are also told in the passage that in order for a molecule to be a stereomer, it must have at least one stereocenter carbon – one with 4 different groups attached.

STEP 3 = > Use the relevant data to solve the question
Examining all three molecules, you can see that they are the same except for the direction of the bonds. You have to determine the stereocenters, then prioritize and finally assign rotation. The correct answer is B and the rotations are shown below. *Remember, carbon 1 will be the carbonyl carbon.

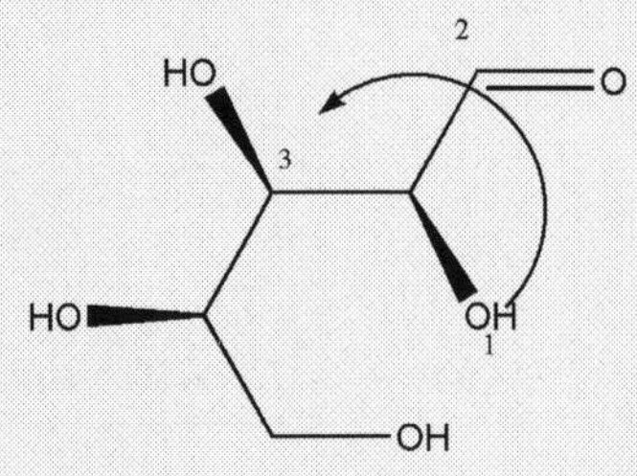

2S

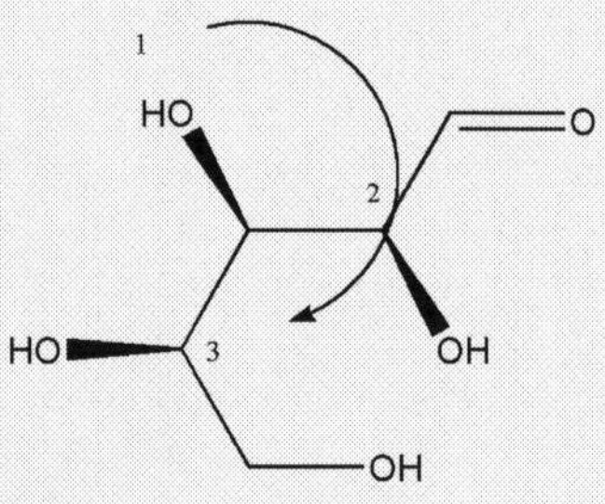

3R

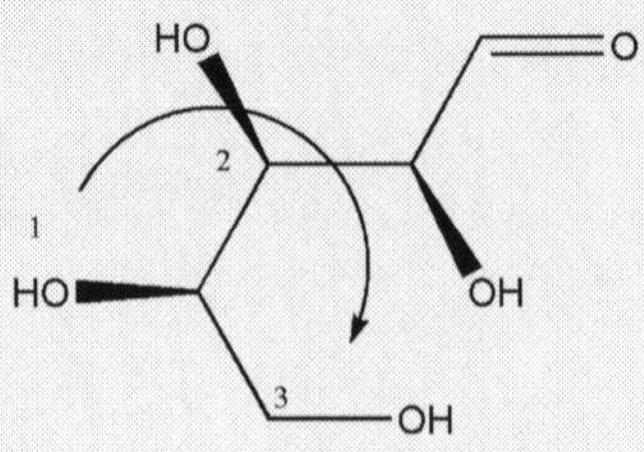

4R

UNIT 11

Questions 37–41

Question 37

STEP 1 = > What do you need to determine to solve the problem?
The question requires you to calculate the degrees of unsaturation in the molecule shown. To do so, you must understand what degrees of unsaturation represent structurally.

STEP 2 = > What relevant data provided in this problem is necessary in order to answer the question?
The passage indicates that each π bond and ring represents a single degree of unsaturation.

STEP 3 = > Use the relevant data to solve the question
The structure drawn contains two rings and two double bonds, so it has four degrees of unsaturation.

Question 38

STEP 1 = > What do you need to determine to solve the problem?
The question requires you to identify the structure with exactly three degrees of unsaturation. To do so, you must determine the unsaturation of each structure.

STEP 2 = > What relevant data provided in this problem is necessary in order to answer the question?
The passage indicates that each π bond and ring represents a single degree of unsaturation.

STEP 3 = > Use the relevant data to solve the question
According to the passage, Choice A has two degrees of unsaturation, Choice B has four, and Choice C has four, but Choice D has exactly three degrees of unsaturation: one double bond and two rings.

Question 39

STEP 1 = > What do you need to determine to solve the problem?
The question requires you to calculate the degrees of unsaturation in the formula given.
To do so, you must apply the formula given in the passage.

STEP 2 = > What relevant data provided in this problem is necessary in order to answer the question?
The passage indicates that the unsaturation of a formula is equal to two times the number of carbon atoms plus the number of nitrogen atoms plus two, minus the number of hydrogens and halogens, all divided by two.

STEP 3 = > Use the relevant data to solve the question
The formula $C_7H_5N_3O_6$ contains $[(7\times2)+3+2-5]/2 = 7$ degrees of unsaturation.
The oxygen atoms do not count in the formula.

Question 40

STEP 1 = > What do you need to determine to solve the problem?
The question requires you to identify the formula containing exactly two degrees of unsaturation.
To do so, you must calculate the unsaturation of each formula.

STEP 2 = > What relevant data provided in this problem is necessary in order to answer the question?
The passage indicates that the unsaturation of a formula is equal to two times the number of carbon atoms plus the number of nitrogen atoms plus two, minus the number of hydrogens and halogens, all divided by two.

STEP 3 = > Use the relevant data to solve the question
Formula A has no unsaturation, Formula C has one degree of unsaturation, and Formula D has one degree of unsaturation, but Formula B has exactly two degrees of unsaturation, $[(7\times2)+1+2-13]/2$.

Question 41

STEP 1 = > What do you need to determine to solve the problem?
The question requires you to determine the number of different unsaturated molecules that can be formed with the given formula. To do so, you must identify all possible structural isomers of the formula.

STEP 2 = > What relevant data provided in this problem is necessary in order to answer the question?
The passage indicates that a saturated structure has no rings or double bonds, so the structures must vary only in branching.

STEP 3 = > Use the relevant data to solve the question
The formula C_6H_{14} can be arranged into the following distinct forms: hexane, 2-methylpentane, 3-methylpentane, 2,3-dimethylbutane, and 2,2-dimethylbutane. Therefore, there are 5 possible structures for the formula C_6H_{14}.

UNIT 12

Questions 42–46

Question 42

STEP 1 = > What do you need to determine to solve the problem?
The question requires you to identify the most likely structure for the cyanate ion. To do so, you must understand what affects the electron distribution in the ion.

STEP 2 = > What relevant data provided in this problem is necessary in order to answer the question?
The passage indicates that in cases where formal charges are unavoidable, such as in ions, electronegativity controls electron distribution.

STEP 3 = > Use the relevant data to solve the question
Cyanate ion [OCN]⁻ possible Lewis Dot structures;

A   B

When two proposed Lewis formulas have the same magnitude of formal charges, choose the one having the negative formal charge on the more electronegative atom.

Oxygen is right of nitrogen on the periodic table, and since electronegativity increases as you go up and to the right, oxygen is more electronegative than nitrogen.

Question 43

STEP 1 = > What do you need to determine to solve the problem?
The question requires you to identify the molecule that cannot be drawn without formal charge.
To do so, you must draw the Lewis structures of each to determine if formal charge is unavoidable in the molecule.

STEP 2 = > What relevant data provided in this problem is necessary in order to answer the question?
The passage indicates that the number of electrons in the structure is equal to the total valence electrons of the atoms in the structure plus the charge of the species, and that they are distributed in bonding pairs and lone pairs.
Also, formal charge for an atom is calculated by subtracting the number of unshared electrons and the number of bonding pairs from the valence number of the atom.

STEP 3 = > Use the relevant data to solve the question
H_2SO_4 can be drawn without formal charge, as the sulfur center can have six bonds, two double bonds to oxygen and two to hydroxyl groups.
CH_3Br can be drawn without formal charge, as a halogen-substituted methane molecule.
O_2 can be drawn as a simple double-bonded molecule with no formal charge. However, O_3 must have formal charge, as the 18 valence electrons must be arranged to place a positive charge on the central oxygen and a negative charge distributed on the terminal atoms.

Question 44

STEP 1 = > What do you need to determine to solve the problem?
The question requires you to identify the H-O-H bond angle in a water molecule.
To do so, you must determine the geometry of the water molecule.

STEP 2 = > What relevant data provided in this problem is necessary in order to answer the question?
The passage indicates that the geometry is based on the number of bonded atoms and lone pairs as described in the table.

STEP 3 = > Use the relevant data to solve the question
The electronic structure of water reveals that the central oxygen atom has two bonds, one to each hydrogen atom, and two lone pairs.
This combination is described in the table as "bent", with 109° bond angles from the base tetrahedral geometry.

Question 45

STEP 1 = > What do you need to determine to solve the problem?
The question requires you to identify the geometry of the perchlorate ion, ClO_4^-.
To do so, you must examine the electronic structure of the ion.

STEP 2 = > What relevant data provided in this problem is necessary in order to answer the question?
The passage indicates that the geometry is based on the number of bonded atoms and lone pairs as described in the table.

STEP 3 = > Use the relevant data to solve the question
The electronic structure of the perchlorate ion reveals a central chlorine with three double bonds to oxygen atoms and a single bond to an oxygen atom, which has a negative formal charge.

The chlorine, with four bonded atoms, has tetrahedral geometry as described in the table. There are actually 7 bonding pairs, counting the double bonds, but for the purposes of geometry only the number of bonds counts, irrespective of bond order.

Question 46

STEP 1 = > What do you need to determine to solve the problem?
The question requires you to identify the molecule that does not obey the octet rule.
To do so, you must examine the electronic structure of the molecules.

STEP 2 = > What relevant data provided in this problem is necessary in order to answer the question?
The passage indicates that the number of electrons in the structure is equal to the total valence electrons of the atoms in the structure plus the charge of the species, and that they are distributed in bonding pairs and lone pairs.
Also, electronegativity plays a role in determining the distribution of electron pairs.

STEP 3 = > Use the relevant data to solve the question

For BF_3 in which the B atom is surrounded by 6 electrons so it does not obey the octet rule. In order to obey the octet rule there would have to be a double bond between B and F. But as F is more electronegative than B, a double bond between B and F would mean that the negative charge would be in the B atom which would destabilize the structure. So the answer is C.

SOLUTIONS - PHYSICS

UNIT 1

Questions 1–5

Question 1

STEP 1 = > What do you need to determine to solve the problem?
The question requires you to identify the β+ particle. To do so, you must determine what its properties are.

STEP 2 = > What relevant data provided in this problem is necessary in order to answer the question?
The passage indicates that the β- particle is an electron, and that the β+ particle has a similar mass but an opposite charge.

STEP 3 = > Use the relevant data to solve the question
A proton is a nuclear particle with positive charge but much more mass than an electron; a neutron has no charge and is comparatively massive; a neutrino is tiny but has no charge. A positron is the electron's antiparticle, with the same mass but opposite charge, and is the β+ particle.

Question 2

STEP 1 = > What do you need to determine to solve the problem?
The question requires you to match the α particle to an atomic nucleus.
To do so, you must determine what the α particle is composed of.

STEP 2 = > What relevant data provided in this problem is necessary in order to answer the question?
The passage indicates that the α particle is composed of two protons and two neutrons.

STEP 3 = > Use the relevant data to solve the question
The hydrogen nucleus is simply a single proton; deuterium is a hydrogen isotope with one proton and one neutron, and tritium is an isotope with one proton and two neutrons. Helium nuclei have two protons and two neutrons, and are identical to α particles.

Question 3

STEP 1 = > What do you need to determine to solve the problem?
The question requires you to identify the product of an alpha decay reaction.
To do so, you must determine how a nucleus changes during alpha decay.

STEP 2 = > What relevant data provided in this problem is necessary in order to answer the question?
The passage indicates that the emitted α particle is two protons and two neutrons, which in nuclear nomenclature is a $^{4}_{2}$He nucleus.

STEP 3 = > Use the relevant data to solve the question
The change in the parent nucleus must be equal to the lost α particle, so the mass number must decrease by four and the atomic number must decrease by two.
Starting from plutonium-242, this means that the alpha decay daughter nucleus must be uranium-238.

Question 4

STEP 1 = > What do you need to determine to solve the problem?
The question requires you to identify the form of electromagnetic radiation that is closest to γ particles.

STEP 2 = > What relevant data provided in this problem is necessary in order to answer the question?
The passage indicates that gamma decay produces gamma rays, a form of very high-energy electromagnetic radiation.

STEP 3 = > Use the relevant data to solve the question
Radio waves are low-frequency, low-energy electromagnetic waves, while visible light has medium frequency and wavelength. Microwaves are more energetic than the visible spectrum, but x-rays are the second-most energetic form of electromagnetic waves, after gamma rays themselves. Therefore, x-rays are the closest in energy to gamma radiation.

Question 5

STEP 1 = > What do you need to determine to solve the problem?
The question requires you to identify the mass number of a beta decay product. To do so, you must determine what changes in a beta decay reaction.

STEP 2 = > What relevant data provided in this problem is necessary in order to answer the question?
The passage indicates that beta decay is the conversion of a proton to a neutron or vice versa, accompanied by the emission of an electron or positron to offset the change in charge.
A β+ or positron emission indicates that the change was from proton to neutron, meaning that the change was from proton to neutron in the nucleus.

STEP 3 = > Use the relevant data to solve the question
Since a proton and a neutron have the same mass in the nucleus, and the emitted positron has negligible mass by comparison, the atomic mass number will not change even though the atomic number has decreased by one.
Therefore, the mass of the nucleus is still 252.

UNIT 2

Questions 6–10

Question 6

STEP 1 = > What do you need to determine to solve the problem?
The question requires you to identify the color of star that has the given physical properties. To do so, you must understand how to read the Hertzsprung-Russell diagram.

STEP 2 = > What relevant data provided in this problem is necessary in order to answer the question?
The passage indicates that the diagram is organized by temperature across the horizontal axis and by luminosity along the vertical axis.

STEP 3 = > Use the relevant data to solve the question
Locating the given temperature places the star in Class B and the low luminosity identifies it as a dwarf, below the main sequence stars.
Therefore, the star will be white.

Question 7

STEP 1 = > What do you need to determine to solve the problem?
The question requires you to identify the densest type of star.
To do so, you must know what each type of star is and what it is composed of.

STEP 2 = > What relevant data provided in this problem is necessary in order to answer the question?
The diagram indicates that the largest stars are the supergiants, which are much brighter and more massive than any other star.

STEP 3 = > Use the relevant data to solve the question
When supergiants collapse after their fusion reactions have run their course, they form either neutron stars or black holes.
Neutron stars pack the mass of a supergiant star into a body 10-20 km across, far denser than any non-singularity object in the universe. Neutron stars are by far the densest stars.

Question 8

STEP 1 = > What do you need to determine to solve the problem?
The question requires you to calculate the approximate life span of a star.
To do so, you must convert its mass and rate of fusion into an estimated life expectancy.

STEP 2 = > What relevant data provided in this problem is necessary in order to answer the question?
The passage indicates that stars are powered for the vast majority of their life cycle by fusing hydrogen, the primary element in their initial composition.

STEP 3 = > Use the relevant data to solve the question
The rate of fusion can be multiplied by 3600, the number of seconds in an hour, to give $2x10^{16}$ kg/hour.
Multiplying this value by 24 gives $5x10^{17}$ kg/day, and multiplying again by 365 gives $2x10^{20}$ kg/year. Dividing the initial mass of the star by this rate gives an estimated lifespan of $2x10^{30}/2x10^{20} = 1x10^{10}$ or 10 billion years.

Question 9

STEP 1 = > What do you need to determine to solve the problem?
The question requires you to identify the product of the nuclear fusion of hydrogen.
To do so, you must understand the process of fusion that takes place in a star's core.

STEP 2 = > What relevant data provided in this problem is necessary in order to answer the question?
The passage indicates that stars fuse hydrogen, converting huge amounts of matter into energy in the process.
The hydrogen is fused into heavier elements, dropping in energy as it goes.

STEP 3 = > Use the relevant data to solve the question
Oxygen, carbon, and iron are created during nuclear fusion, but only in the latter stages of the stellar life cycle.
The primary product of the hydrogen fusion taking place in main sequence stars is helium.

Question 10

STEP 1 = > What do you need to determine to solve the problem?
The question requires you to calculate the absolute magnitude of a star.
To do so, you must apply the formula given in the passage.

STEP 2 = > What relevant data provided in this problem is necessary in order to answer the question?
The passage indicates that the absolute magnitude of a star is dependent on its apparent magnitude and the log of its distance in parsecs from the Earth.

STEP 3 = > Use the relevant data to solve the question
Canopus has an apparent magnitude of -0.72, and is 96 parsecs (300 light-years) from the Earth.
The log of 96 can be accurately estimated to be 2, meaning that the absolute magnitude of the star is very nearly $-0.72 - 5 \times (2 - 1) = -5.72$, or about -5.5.

UNIT 3

Questions 11–15

Question 11

STEP 1 = > What do you need to determine to solve the problem?
The question requires you to calculate the total resistance of the given circuit.
To do so, you must understand how resistances combine within series and parallel circuits.

STEP 2 = > What relevant data provided in this problem is necessary in order to answer the question?
The passage indicates that the resistances of resistors in series add up to the total resistance, while resistors in parallel do so in a reciprocal fashion.

STEP 3 = > Use the relevant data to solve the question
The resistance of the two parallel resistors can be calculated using the equation $1/R = 1/R1 + 1/R2$.
Plugging in 3 Ω for R1 and R2 gives $1/R = 1/3 + 1/3$ or $1/R = 2/3$. Therefore, the parallel resistors are equivalent to a single resistor of 1.5 Ω. This equivalent resistor, when added to the resistor in series, gives a total circuit resistance of 3 Ω + 1.5 Ω = 4.5 Ω.

Question 12

STEP 1 = > What do you need to determine to solve the problem?
The question requires you to calculate the potential difference in a DC circuit.
To do so, you must apply Ohm's Law.

STEP 2 = > What relevant data provided in this problem is necessary in order to answer the question?
The passage indicates that the voltage drop is equal to the current times the resistance.

STEP 3 = > Use the relevant data to solve the question
Since $V = I \times R$, the potential difference is 2 A x 8 Ω = 16 V.

Question 13

STEP 1 = > What do you need to determine to solve the problem?
The question requires you to calculate the current flowing through a DC circuit.
To do so, you must first determine the resistance, then apply Ohm's Law.

STEP 2 = > What relevant data provided in this problem is necessary in order to answer the question?
The passage indicates that resistors in series add linearly, and that current is determined by resistance and voltage in accordance with Ohm's Law.

STEP 3 = > Use the relevant data to solve the question
The two $1 \, \Omega$ resistors have an equivalent resistance of $R = 1 \, \Omega + 1 \, \Omega = 2 \, \Omega$.
Since $V = I \times R$, the current is equal to $I = V/R = 10 \, V / 2 \, \Omega = 5 \, A$.

Question 14

STEP 1 = > What do you need to determine to solve the problem?
The question requires you to calculate the energy flowing through a circuit from the current and resistance.
To do so, you must calculate the power of the circuit.

STEP 2 = > What relevant data provided in this problem is necessary in order to answer the question?
The passage indicates that the power is equal to the current times the voltage, which is equal to current times resistance.

STEP 3 = > Use the relevant data to solve the question
Since $P = I \times V$ and $V = I \times R$, then $P = I2 \times R$. Therefore, $P = (20 \, A)2 \times 5 \, \Omega = 2000 \, W$, which is equal to 2000 J/s. In one second, the circuit carries 2000 J of electrical energy.

Question 15

STEP 1 = > What do you need to determine to solve the problem?
The question requires you to calculate the resistance of three resistors in parallel.
To do so, you must understand how resistors in parallel work.

STEP 2 = > What relevant data provided in this problem is necessary in order to answer the question?
The passage indicates that resistors in parallel add reciprocally, and that voltage is the product of current and resistance.

STEP 3 = > Use the relevant data to solve the question
Ohm's Law, V = I x R, means that the total resistance is R = V/I = 12 V/6 A = 2 Ω.
Since the three resistors in parallel are identical, the equivalent resistance equation is 1/2 =
1/R + 1/R + 1/R = 3/R, so R must equal 6, and the resistors all have a resistance of 6 Ω.

UNIT 4

Questions 16–20

Question 16

STEP 1 = > What do you need to determine to solve the problem?
The question requires you to calculate the image distance for a lens.
To do so, you must apply optical geometry to the lens.

STEP 2 = > What relevant data provided in this problem is necessary in order to answer
the question?
The passage indicates that the reciprocals of the image and object distances add to the
reciprocal of the focal length.

STEP 3 = > Use the relevant data to solve the question
Since the focal length is 50 cm and the object distance is 100 cm and the lens obeys the
equation 1/f = 1/o + 1/i, the image distance can be calculated by 1/i = 1/f – 1/o = 1/50 –
1/100 = 1/100.
Therefore, the image distance is 100 cm.

Question 17

STEP 1 = > What do you need to determine to solve the problem?
The question requires you to calculate the magnification of an image.
To do so, you must calculate the object distance of the lens.

STEP 2 = > What relevant data provided in this problem is necessary in order to answer
the question?
The passage indicates that the magnification is the ratio of the size of the image to the
object.

STEP 3 = > Use the relevant data to solve the question
The object distance can be calculated by 1/o = 1/f – 1/i = 1/30 – 1/45 = 1/90, giving an
object distance of 90 mm.
The magnification can be calculated by M = - i/o = - 45/90 = -0.5.

Question 18

STEP 1 = > What do you need to determine to solve the problem?
The question requires you to identify the type of image produced from the last question.
To do so, you must understand what the difference is between the types of image.

STEP 2 = > What relevant data provided in this problem is necessary in order to answer the question?
The passage indicates that a positive magnification means the image is upright, while a negative magnification means the image is inverted.
An image on the same side of the lens as the object is virtual, while an image on the opposite side is real.

STEP 3 = > Use the relevant data to solve the question
The convex lens produces a convergent image on the opposite side of the lens, producing a real image, and the negative magnification makes it an inverted image.

Question 19

STEP 1 = > What do you need to determine to solve the problem?
The question requires you to calculate the speed of light in water.
To do so, you must understand the concept of the refraction index.

STEP 2 = > What relevant data provided in this problem is necessary in order to answer the question?
The passage indicates that a material's index of refraction represents the ratio of the speed of light in vacuum to the seed of light in the material.

STEP 3 = > Use the relevant data to solve the question
The index of refraction is calculated by $n = c/v$, where c is the speed of light in vacuum or 300,000 km/s, so the speed of light in water is $v = c/n = 300,000/1.33 = 225,000$ km/s.

Question 20

STEP 1 = > What do you need to determine to solve the problem?
The question requires you to calculate the index of refraction of glass.
To do so, you must understand the concept of the refraction index.

STEP 2 = > What relevant data provided in this problem is necessary in order to answer the question?
The passage indicates that a material's index of refraction represents the ratio of the speed of light in vacuum to the seed of light in the material.

STEP 3 = > Use the relevant data to solve the question
Since $n = c/v$, the index of refraction of glass is $n = 300,000/200,000 = 1.5$.